T0367937

THE FIRST
AFRICAN AMERICAN
SAMURAI

THE FIRST
AFRICAN AMERICAN
SAMURAI

TYRONE R. AIKEN, MSPM

This book is a work of non-fiction. Unless otherwise noted, the author and the publisher make no explicit guarantees as to the accuracy of the information contained in this book and in some cases, names of people and places have been altered to protect their privacy.

Archway Publishing books may be ordered through booksellers or by contacting:

Archway Publishing
1663 Liberty Drive
Bloomington, IN 47403
www.archwaypublishing.com
844-669-3957

Because of the dynamic nature of the Internet, any web addresses or links contained in this book may have changed since publication and may no longer be valid. The views expressed in this work are solely those of the author and do not necessarily reflect the views of the publisher, and the publisher hereby disclaims any responsibility for them.

Any people depicted in stock imagery provided by Getty Images are models, and such images are being used for illustrative purposes only.
Certain stock imagery © Getty Images.

ISBN: 978-1-6657-5809-3 (sc)
ISBN: 978-1-6657-5811-6 (hc)
ISBN: 978-1-6657-5810-9 (e)

Library of Congress Control Number: 2024905416

Print information available on the last page.

Archway Publishing rev. date: 05/10/2024

The First African American Samurai

As you read this book the images and narratives might tempt you to simulate techniques and concepts. We warn readers not to attempt or encourage or to apply any techniques or tactics within. The type of knowledge required cannot be gained without instruction from a qualified teacher. Specifically, the author and publishers are not rendering or providing professional advice or services for readers.

The ideas, propositions, and methods provided in this book are not a substitute for training under a qualified instructor. "In fact, the publisher and the author shall not be held liable or responsible for any loss or damage or injury allegedly occurring from any suggestion or information contained in this book."

Tyrone Aiken
2-23-2024

PREFACE

The purpose of this book is to encourage a deeper understanding of martial arts as a lifestyle dedicated to service and character development. The word Samurai means to serve.

ACKNOWLEDGMENT

I would like to thank my colleagues, family, and students who inspired me to tirelessly work to transform passions, pursuits, and aspirations into an inspiring story. A special thanks is due to Brunella Costagliola at Kevin Anderson and Associates.

INTRODUCTION

Verba volant, scripta manent.

These four Latin words convey the entire purpose of this book: spoken words fly away, written words will remain. John Womble wasn't a man of many words, but he was the kind of man everyone listened to when he spoke because his words carried weight and had been carefully chosen among his vast and rich vocabulary. The first Black American Samurai, he was a *sensei* (Japanese word that refers to a martial arts teacher) to many of us. But his teachings went far beyond the *dōjō* (a room in which people practice martial arts) and they branched out into every aspect of life.

Attending Womble's martial arts classes actually had little to do with martial arts—at least the sport usually seen in tournaments, where people's highest aspiration is to earn one more trophy or medal to add to their collection. To Womble, martial arts tournament medals and trophies had no value if his students hadn't achieved the mental fortitude that it takes to be a true Samurai. He stood against the capitalistic mindset that drives many to seek instant gratification in the form of prestigious black belts and shiny trophies, and instead championed the idea of studying martial arts for its philosophy and way of life that would eventually develop into the solid and reliable mindset of a Samurai.

Womble was a true Samurai just like his sensei, Dr. Tsuyoshi Chitose. He was only nineteen years old when he earned his place in the school (in Japanese, *ryu*) of Samurai in Kumamoto City, Japan, where he had been stationed with the US Army. Dr. Chitose was his primary sensei along with eleven others, including the headmaster of the ryu, Gōgen Yamaguchi. A para-ranger, Womble had left the racially segregated United States of America in 1954 and sent to the Land of the Rising Sun during the Korean War. It was under Dr. Chitose's guidance that Womble learned what it truly means to be a Samurai and how hard it was to gain two of the most important skills a martial artist must possess: mindfulness and spiritual awareness. But gain them he did, and he graduated summa cum laude, received a golden sword and marks on his upper forearms to identify his status, and was presented with a Menkyo (license) for a second-degree black belt in judo.

When he came back to the United States of America, Womble brought with him the invaluable experience he had gained overseas and began sharing his knowledge of the Samurai *modus vivendi* (way of life) with those who wished to learn, focusing not just on the physical, but especially on the mental and spiritual development of his students, in order to foster the solid tradition of loyalty, devotion, and strength that found its roots in ancient Japan. Given his many achievements in Japan and in the US Armed Forces, Womble could have easily chosen to monetize his accolades and live a life of fame and fortune. Instead, he chose to teach martial arts to inner-city students because he knew that he could offer them a proven and reliable method to channel energy into something positive and eventually help them become productive citizens and problem-solvers. His students came from different cultural and religious backgrounds, but Womble provided them with a safe space in which they realized that their identities were an asset, not a deterrent. Born in many countries in Africa, Asia, Europe, and South America, they flourished in his university courses even as they faced racism and prejudice in others. By helping them see the power and strength in their own uniqueness, Womble guided them through the many challenges that growing up in the inner cities of the United States of America and other countries threw at them on a daily basis, from racism to corruption. After all, one of the main purposes of educating students, especially at a collegiate level, is to guide them to a more worldly vision and attitude, a comprehension and appreciation for other cultures and ways of life.

Of course, there were setbacks and failures, but Womble did not respond to them with denial, excuses, nor regret. He simply showed his students that, no matter how many times they fell, they had no other choice but to get right back up from the mat, both the physical one of the dōjō and, most importantly, the metaphorical one of life. Womble knew that if they harnessed the power of the immovable mind, they would be able to step out of the dōjō and walk through life with their head held high as they fought against crime, violence, and systemic racism.

His students, such as the ones who have authored this book, are Womble's ultimate legacy, championing their sensei's firm belief that "Character is what you do when no one is watching." As a highly trained warrior, both as a Samurai and as an army ranger, Womble strived to teach his students how to uphold exceptional standards of character and be seekers of peace even though they had been trained to be ready for war. To the sensei, being a role model to others meant to act honorably and be loyal, even while living in a society that at times rewards corruption, dishonesty, and racism. Many of his students have embraced their sensei's teachings and absorbed his vast knowledge of what being a true Samurai means and have gone into the world to apply the lessons learned. Many of them have made their voices heard to the government and fought tirelessly in order to change outdated preconceptions, traditions, and rules. They have given back to their communities and provided them with tangible help as well as moral and emotional support and guidance. They have taken successful steps toward fighting systemic corruption and racism, even when their own lives were in danger because of the countless protests that precipitated serious threats made against them, their families, and their work.

Just like Womble's classes were not "how to kick and punch adversaries so as to win medals and trophies," this is not a how-to book or instruction manual on how to attack and win over powerful and dangerous opponents. There are no photos or videos with collaborative participants encouraging you to believe that practicing in a controlled environment for a few months will prepare you to face hostile attacks in an unfamiliar environment (most law enforcement and military experts know that they have to keep training so to keep their skills sharp). Also, while martial arts have the potential to help students learn how to defend themselves, this book does not include tips or tricks on how to get yourself out of situations where the attacker has a gun, knife, or chemicals, nor are there suggestions on what to do if you find yourself in the presence of an attacker at your home, workplace, or church.

What this book does is share Womble's exceptional life and teachings to those interested in learning about martial arts—the way of life, not the sport. But most importantly, by sharing Womble's knowledge, this book goes behind the kicks and punches and dives deep into the spirit of the Samurai to unveil what it really takes to be steady and calm while surrounded by conflict and chaos. We will tune out the screeching shouts to explore and explain how to achieve a Samurai's most important weapon: the immovable mind. With each chapter, you will get closer to understanding how to harness the ability to sustain mental and physical health through martial arts. In doing so, you will be equipped to build, manage, and optimize a personal program that caters to your needs and expectations, while researching the ideas within to develop life strategies based on assessments as opposed to assumptions, because this book will push you to question what you believe to be facts. Sometimes, what we believe to be fact is just an opinion; and when we act based on beliefs that turn out to be false, we get in trouble. This book encourages you to question yourself, question life, and question your beliefs. It's only by asking "What if?" that we learn and grow. It's only by challenging the status quo that real change happens.

However, in order to learn how to harness the power of the Samurai modus vivendi and become productive citizens of today, we must understand what happened yesterday. That is the reason this book digs into the historical and political context that framed Womble's journey to Japan and his way back to the United States of America. You will learn of the role of the Samurai and how it evolved throughout the many dynasties that ruled over Japan, though the core principles of what it means to be a Samurai have remained the same for centuries. But most of all, you will learn of the first Black American Samurai, who lived his life quietly but effectively, and the invaluable knowledge he shared with his students—knowledge that he *spoke* to many of us, but since spoken words fly away, as a tribute to our sensei we have chosen to translate his legacy into written words, as they shall remain.

ONE

In 1954, when nineteen-year-old John Womble left a racially seg-regated United States of America as a para-ranger for the US Army to be stationed at Camp Wood in Kumamoto, Japan, the American perception of Japanese culture had been severely affected by the anti-Japanese propaganda that had taken over the country a decade prior, during World War II. The Japanese people had been portrayed as savages, "mere prints off the same photographic negative, devoid of individuality,"[1] unable to think for themselves as they mindlessly obeyed Emperor Hirohito; their popular Samurai class was comprised of nothing more than disciplined killers.

However, when the young Black soldier began his life in the country of the Rising Sun, he didn't meet the same violent and de-humanized people that the anti-Japanese propaganda had tried hard to sell—much like he himself didn't fit the stereotypical representa-tion of the dangerous, illiterate, and immature Black man that many American corporations of the time depicted through their ridicule of Black people's appearance and behavior, plastering the caricatures on everything from cereal boxes to detergent to wall hangings.

---

[1] John W. Dower, "War Without Mercy: Race and Power in the Pacific War." (New York: Pantheon Books, 1987): 30.

1

Instead, the young soldier found a country with longstanding traditions, a sense of pride that dated back centuries, and a history that highlighted the importance of the country's core values. He witnessed firsthand where part of Japan's pride came from when he attended a boxing match between a Black boxer—who had traveled all the way from the United States—and a Japanese karate expert.

At the time, boxing was source of great pride for African Americans as it was one of the very first sports to be desegregated and turn African Americans into boxing legends, both at home and abroad. First among them, Joe Louis distinguished himself when, in 1938, he defeated Max Schmeling, boxing champion of Nazi Germany. After losing the first match, which lasted twelve rounds, Louis knocked Schmeling out in one round, in the second match. Prompting white America to cheer for a man who had clearly defied and broken racial barriers under Jim Crow laws. Louis's undisputed victory over Germany's symbol of Aryan supremacy convinced white Americans to see him as a national hero and symbol of American democracy, as opposed to classifying him as a dangerous, uncontrollable Black American. At the beginning of his career, his managers had instructed Louis to please white America by not "gloat[ing] over opponents. He could not be seen in public with white women. He had to be seen as a Bible-reading, mother-loving, God-fearing individual, and not to be 'too black.'"[2] In 1951, Joe Lewis put on an impressive display of his skills during several exhibitions in Japan.[3]

---

[2] Jeffrey Sammons, "The Fight" transcript. http://www.shoppbs.pbs.org/wgbh/amex/fight/filmmore/pt.html

[3] Joe Koizumi_Today (November 18) is the sixty-ninth anniversary of "Brown Bomber" Joe Louis coming to show an exhibition in Japan in 1951 https://fightnews.com/69th-anniversary-of-joe-louis-exhibition-in-japan/92423

After being impressed even more by Lewis, he was sure that his hometown boxer would defeat his opponent in a few rounds. He thought to himself, *this is going to be a slam dunk and should win against the five-foot tall Japanese martial artist in no time.* Womble couldn't believe his eyes when he witnessed the Japanese combatant evade punches for several rounds and finally end the contest with a single blow to the abdomen. The boxer seemed to be frozen upright and eventually keeled over. John Womble looked on in awe as his boxer suffered defeat at the hands of the Japanese karate fighter. As surprise and shock spread across his face, he turned to his Japanese associates and asked, "Who is he?"

Their one-word answer was: "Samurai."

This word would completely change Womble's life and shape his future.

Determined to learn more, he eventually became a student of Dr. Tsuyoshi Chitose, who came from a lineage of martial artists in Okinawa and had founded the Chitō-ryū, a Japanese style of karate that combined Dr. Chitose's knowledge of physiology with karate techniques to avoid excessive physical strain to the martial artists. The relationship between the nineteen-year-old Womble, who was still actively serving in the US Army, and Dr. Chitose, allowed the young paratrooper to become one of five hundred candidates who trained at the School of Samurai, which was managed by twelve masters—polymaths with exceptional knowledge of Bujutsu and budō.[4] It's important to know that colored belts and sashes became popular because of imitations of Dr. Kanō's efforts to motivate Japanese

---

[4] The parent systems of budō or martial sports is called Bujutsu, the older system of combat that is not legal to practice outside of military and law enforcement in many countries as it used deadly force to maim or kill with dangerous blows, choke holds, and poison darts.

children to enjoy judo. Prior practices of traditional martial arts schools and temples didn't include the multi colors of belts used in commercial martial sports. They used marks on the body and special artifacts and authentic weapons as recognition of accomplishment. In addition, hidden knowledge of systems was transmitted and served as credentials within the world of traditional martial arts. That's why, upon graduation from the School of Samurai, he received a golden sword and marks on his upper forearms to identify his status. In addition, Chitose presented Womble with a Menkyo imprinted with his Hanko/Inkan (stamp) with comments in Japanese and cosigned by his commanding officer—Captain John Blish for a second-degree black belt for judo, which is how he became the judo teacher at Camp Wood.

Womble successfully embraced the Samurai modus vivendi and embarked on an exceptional journey of physical, mental, and spiritual development that echoed a solid tradition of loyalty, devotion, and strength that found its beginning many centuries prior, during a time known as the Heian period.

It was during the Heian period (794–1185) that the figure of the Samurai came to be. The Samurai started as armed supporters of leading landowners whose lineage and heritage were traced to the imperial family—meaning they were thought to be of divine origin. The word Samurai derives from the Japanese *saburau*, which translates to "serve." Although the Samurai is usually depicted holding a sword, his first weapon was a bow and arrow, mainly because Samurai could rarely rely on swords because they broke often.

That is, at least, until 700 BCE—according to legend—when swordsmiths Amakuni and his son Amakura built the strongest and most perfect swords for the emperor and his warriors to use in battle. It all began when the father and son duo saw soldiers come back from battle with broken swords. The emperor, who had joined his troops, walked by Amakuni and Amakura but didn't offer them any sign of recognition. Deeply mortified for failing the warriors and their emperor by providing them with weak and faulty weapons, Amakuni and his son prayed to the Shinto gods for seven days and seven nights, vowing to build unbreakable swords. After many days of hard and intense work, the swordsmiths built a single-edged sword with a curvature. Most swords at the time were straight. The curved blade was somewhat of an innovation in weaponry at the time. The curved blade redefined Japanese swordsmanship at the time. The blade also fit on auxiliary weapons or polearms like the naginata.[5] The cutting inward plus thrusting gave a Samurai on horseback an advantage in striking enemies on the ground. The weapon never failed their emperor nor the soldiers ever again.

The sword holds deep spiritual meaning to its swordsmith and Samurai. It was actually during this same period that swordsmiths started following a sacred ritual, during which they vowed to commit their spirit to the forging and tempering of the steel. With this commitment, the sword would then be passed on to the Samurai, whose soul was believed to be held forever within the sword. Many of the old Samurai swords cannot be replicated by modern technology because the method in which they were made are closely guarded and protected, as they are considered national treasures. Many Japanese

---

[5]   https://www.quora.com/How-does-the-naginata-compare-to-the-halberd#:~:text=.The%20naginata%20is%20a%20Japanese%20weapon%20that%20typically%20has%20a%20curved%2C%20single%2Dedged%20blade%20and%20a%20long%20handle.%20It%20was%20traditionally%20used%20by%20samurai%20on%20horseback%20as%20a%20way%20to%20strike%20at%20mounted%20opponents%2C%20but%20it%20was%20also%20used%20by%20foot%20soldiers.

swords are in foreign museums and even though they were created hundreds of years ago, they are still as sharp as razors.

The sword became an even more important staple in the life of a Samurai when, beginning in the tenth century, Japan became a feudal society ruled by the *daimyō* class of lords (*daimyō* meaning "great names") under the direction of an all-powerful shogun— a military commander chosen by the emperor. During this time, law and justice were maintained by the Samurai, who trained in martial arts and *kenjutsu* or "the art of the sword." They were simultaneously imperial guards, local law enforcement, and key players in the constantly shifting alliances of a protracted civil war involving more than a dozen states. Sequestered in the capital of Kyoto, the emperor struggled to maintain control over the provincial territories. As the emperor lost power and became more of a figurehead, the Samurai's position under the shogun was strengthened.

By the time the twelfth century had arrived, rivalry for military power over Japan was in full swing, with the Minamoto and the Taira clans vying for influence over the nation—the Taira clan had been influential over the imperial government, while the Minamoto clan was emerging as a threat to the stability of the Taira[6]. In 1180, the clans engaged in battle, known as the Genpei War, which lasted five years when Minamoto no Yoritomo—the head of the Minamoto clan— rose to power. When Minamoto no Yoritomo established the first *shogun*—military dictatorship—in Kamakura, the Samurai went from warrior class to privileged status and increased political influence and gained a stipend. During the Kamakura jidai or period (1185–1333), China and Japan established cultural ties and China introduced Zen Buddhism to Japan, and the Samurai embraced its philosophical core,

---

[6] The Editors of Encyclopedia Britannia, "Genpei War." https://www.britannica.com/event/Gempei-War

spiritual rituals, and belief that the path to wisdom and peace comes from within. It was also during this period that the code of honor by which they would become known, the *bushido*, was solidified. Selflessness, bravery, high standards of personal conduct, and prowess on the battlefield all emerged as cornerstones of the Samurai lifestyle during this influential time.

The role of the Samurai became even more prominent when the Mongolian Emperor Kublai Khan—grandson of Genghis Khan—invaded Japan. He had already conquered China and Korea—in 1230 and 1231 respectively—and now he had his eyes set on the islands to the east. After sending numerous threats to the Japanese emperor demanding that he submit to the Mongols, Kublai Khan decided to attack when his messages went unanswered. So, he gathered hundreds of thousands of Chinese, Korean, and Mongol troops and ordered a seaborn attack. The first launch occurred in 1274, but most of the Mongols' vessels were destroyed by a powerful typhoon that prevented any of the ships from reaching mainland Japan. Khan, unwilling to yield, planned another attack in 1281, this one even mightier, to ensure the Japanese had no chance at victory. Yet, as the four thousand vessels made their way across the ocean, they faced an even more powerful typhoon, which left the Mongols with no safe escape.

Legend has it that it was the Shinto god of storm, lightning, and thunder, Kaminari—also known as Raijin—who protected Japan by creating a divine wind. In Japanese, the name Kaminari means spirit (or deity) of thunder. It is from that name and its metaphorical meaning that the Japanese people took inspiration to name the kamikaze—who, during World War II, launched the attack on Pearl Harbor, prompting the United States of America to enter the war and contributing to the way Japanese people were then represented to the American public through propaganda—came from: it was said that they embodied the divine wind that had once protected Japan against foreign invasion. It was during the twelfth century that Samurai started to embrace (ritualized) suicide as a way to achieve an honorable death, especially if they were at risk of falling into the enemy's hands. Seppuku—also known as hara-kiri—was a ritual suicide that the Samurai performed. They would first drink sake and pen a poem that celebrated death before stabbing themselves in the stomach and twisting it upward and through the torso to be sure death would come.

Samurais' spiritual beliefs found their roots in Zen Buddhism, Taoism, Shintoism, and Confucianism, as they believed that a blend of these philosophies provided them with the balance necessary for being both warriors and citizens. Knowing the duties of one's station and one's role in society was easier with the morality and correctness that Confucius had taught in China in 500 BCE. The way of the bushido, which advocated loyalty to one's master and respect for superiority, self-discipline, and ethical behavior, was based largely on the teachings of Confucius, which were introduced to Japan in the third century. Confucianism merged seamlessly with the military zeitgeist of Japan during this period. The bushido philosophy is still an undercurrent of everyday life in Japan, dictating work and familial relationships and engendering a law-abiding society of tacit hierarchies. Zen Buddhism and Shintoism, on the other hand, offered spiritual harmony and gave the Samurai strength on the battlefield, encouraging them to be at one with nature, heaven, and even their own mortality.

Christianity was also beginning to gain a toehold by the late 1500s. Missionaries had experienced some success with converting Japanese nobility, and whenever a member of the *daimyō* class became a Christian, he typically pressured those in his sway to convert as well. However, most Samurai saw Christianity as a threat or converted only on paper for the sake of gaining trade advantages with the West. It was a missionary from Italy named Alessandro Vagliano who brought the man who would eventually become the very first African Samurai and the first Samurai of foreign descent to Japan: Yasuke.

Born in Sudan and part of the Dinka people—who lived alongside the Nile in modern day Republic of South Sudan—he was abducted as a child by Indian slave traders, trafficked through the Indian Ocean and forced into slavery as a boy. After meeting Vagliano in India, Yasuke worked as his bodyguard and eventually traveled with him to Japan in 1579. They arrived when the country was waging a brutal civil war that would end twenty-five years later. Yasuke became an immediate sensation, most likely due to his immense stature—he was over six feet tall, which gave him a towering position over shorter Japanese men.

Oda Nobunaga—a daimyō and Samurai who wanted to unify Japan—took a fancy to Yasuke because he had never seen a Black person before. He was also fascinated by Yasuke's engaging personality, his knowledge of many foreign lands, and his ability to speak multiple languages. A month after their meeting, Nobunaga recognized Yasuke's potential and decided to introduce him to the Samurai code and way of life, which he took to quickly. He invited Yasuke to his castle and presented him with a katana as a symbol of his new status as a Samurai. When, in 1582, Nobunaga's Samurai general Akechi attacked the daimyō's residence, Honnō-ji Temple, with hundreds of Samurai and set the lord's residence on fire, Nobunaga realized that his desire to unify Japan could never be achieved and chose seppuku to retain his honor. Legend has it, however, that before going through with seppuku, Nobunaga instructed Yasuke to bring his decapitated head and sword to his son because he didn't want them to fall into enemy hands. After collecting his lord's remains, the loyal Samurai knew he had to get out of the residence before it burned down. As he stepped outside the temple, he met three Samurai whose helmets barely reached his chest. The Samurai were unable to move at the sight of such a mighty warrior, whose height and dark complexion frightened them. Worried that the inferno roaring behind him might stop him from fulfilling the vow he had made to his lord, Yasuke looked down at the frightened Samurai and said, *"Yasuke de gozaru."* I am Yasuke. The African Samurai, now a *ronin*—a Samurai without a master—stepped forward into the night, leaving behind him the legendary story of the abducted boy who, forced into slavery, rose to become one of the most famous Samurai.

During this era, Yasuke's skill with the katana sword became legendary. The weapon was innovative and advanced both in terms of metallurgy and the development of legends and combat systems as it was applied to combat between various clans. Eventually it became the most sophisticated science of sword fighting (Kenjutsu). Even though Nobunaga had adopted them, the use of muskets was not widespread until later, with the arrival of Europeans who then revolutionized warfare for the Samurai; rough handguns from China were used occasionally in battle, but more often, the Samurai were supported by foot soldiers bearing bows and arrows to supplement the *katana*.

Toyotomi Hideyoshi's ascension to power in the sixteenth century was a watershed moment for feudal Japan. A Samurai who exerted tremendous control over the nation by virtue of clever political and military maneuvering, Hideyoshi took his might to new levels, even attempting conquests of Korea and China. But it was his alliance with another Samurai, Tokugawa Ieyasu[7], that changed the course of history for Japan and, ironically, ultimately began the sunset of the warrior class.

---

[7] Tokugawa Ieyasu was the founder of the Tokugawa shogunate, which began in 1603 and ended 1868. While this chapter focuses on the role that Tokugawa Ieyasu himself played in the history of Japan, the mention of Tokugawa in the chapter often refers to the shogunate as a whole and not Ieyasu, the first shogun.

Like most other Samurai, Ieyasu was born into this privileged class. As a young boy, his father sent him as hostage to live with his lord—a way to secure military ties between the Tokugawa family and the Imagawa family—an experience that profoundly affected him but one that also pushed him to focus on his core values and strengthen his spirit. Ieyasu lived for years with this other family, who introduced him to sword training and the rules of war, arts that were frequently taught to males of a similar upbringing. It wasn't until his master was killed in battle that Ieyasu was offered a choice: to remain in the territory where he had been raised or to return to the home of his birth family. Ieyasu chose the latter, aligning himself with none other than Oda Nobunaga; for years, he waited patiently for the right opportunity to make his move and oust Hideyoshi's dynasty, his greatest competitor for power. In the interim, he was sent by Hideyoshi to build a castle in Edo, which later became Tokyo, Japan's capital. Ieyasu married and had many heirs, while Hideyoshi struggled to produce just one, Hideyori.

Once Hideyoshi had been killed in battle in Korea, Tokugawa Ieyasu—who had chosen not to follow Hideyoshi to Korea but remained in Japan—conquered his army, bringing their decapitated heads to Hideyoshi's headquarters as proof and consolidating his vast power. Eventually he even accused Hideyori of subversion and attacked the family castle in Osaka, slaughtering thousands and inciting Hideyori to commit seppuku. This was a move Ieyasu was later thought to have regretted, as he had promised Hideyoshi that he would protect Hideyori and forcing him to die was considered a violation of the Samurai honor code. However, when Ieyasu seized command of the island of Honshu, including the cities of Kyoto, Osaka, and Edo, which were the most vital parts of Japan, this ended the interminable warring between states and centralized the Japanese government. Tokugawa Ieyasu was then awarded the coveted shogunate.

Ieyasu, who had formed a close bond with the Netherlands and perceived Spain and Portugal as threats given their close relationship with Japanese Christian groups and missionaries—who were perceived as a threat to Japan's national unity—closed Japan to most outsiders, expelling foreigners and exiling three hundred Christians to Macao and Manila; he then banned Christianity and espoused neo-Confucianism—a revival of Confucianism, which had been introduced to Japan in the third century BC. Ieyasu believed in mastering the path to personal virtue, which he achieved by studying eastern classics, in particular the *Analects* and other ancient Chinese texts that focused on the Chinese philosopher's beliefs. Confucius believed that "everything we see in this world can be reduced to its simplest essence, which is called *li*.[8] There is purity in everything that we see. But that purity—whether it is the essence of a tree or the essence of an individual—is oftentimes diluted by things in the world that we cannot see, an invisible energy which is called *qi*. Thus, the goal of one's life is to get beyond the qi that might adulterate one's true essence and come to a true realization of the purity and simplicity of our nature, the li."[9] What truly caught Ieyasu's attention, however, was Confucius's belief that the well-being of a country depended on the moral virtues of its leader and people. He strived to embody the virtues he believed a leader should have and, in his testament to two Buddhist priests and Samurai Honda Masazumi, he said: "Life is like walking along a long road shouldering a heavy load; there is no need to hurry. One who treats difficulties as the normal state of affairs will never be discontented. Patience is the source of eternal peace; treat anger as an enemy. Harm will befall one who knows only success

---

[8] The *Analects* are believed to have been written by Confucius' followers.
[9] Shelton Woods, "Religion in Tokugawa Japan," About Japan, a Teacher's Resource. https://aboutjapan.japansociety.org/religion-in-tokugawa-japan

and has never experienced failure. Blame yourself rather than others. It is better not to reach than to go too far."[10] Soon after speaking his testament, which was written by his witnesses, he died in 1616 of stomach cancer.

During the Edo period (1603–1867), also known as the Tokugawa period after the family's name of the shogunate, the merchant class in Japan made tremendous strides, which helped bring renewed prosperity to the country. As the Tokugawa shogunate thrived, so too did the arts, such as Kabuki theatre, puppetry, literature, and printing. The end of this era produced great artists like Hiroshige, who was himself born into a Samurai family. Due to the strong emphasis on neo-Confucianism, the Tokugawa period was based on the belief that social harmony could only be maintained by respecting reciprocal relationships between a dominant figure and an inferior one: "ruler-subject, father-son, husband-wife, older brother-younger brother, and friendships to friend."[11] While the inferior figure was to always look up to its dominant counterpart and follow its example, the dominant figure was always to be benevolent toward its inferior counterpart and work hard to set a great example. As a result, social rankings became more regimented under the Tokugawa shogunate. There were only four recognized classes—Samurai, merchants, artists, and farmers—with almost no mobility between them. While they were still always ready for battle if needed, during peacetime, the Samurai went from primarily performing military service to working as local bureaucrats. During this period, Samurai dressed in a distinc-

---

[10] Precepts of Tokugawa Ieyasu, Shogun of Japan (1603–1616), inscribed at Tosho-gu Shrine, Ueno. http://www.oldtokyo.com/tosho-gu-shrine-ueno-park/

[11] Shelton Woods, "Religion in Tokugawa Japan," About Japan, a Teacher's Resource. https://aboutjapan.japansociety.org/religion-in-tokugawa-japan

tive but dignified fashion that allowed them to be noticed in public. While they wore a kimono of fine cloth at home, they would don a two-piece *kamishimo* over the kimono when leaving the house, which consisted of a sleeveless jacket and trousers. Travel or colder weather often necessitated a jacket with sleeves or a hat. An *obi*, or belt, held the Samurai's swords, and their hair was swept up in a topknot called a *chomage*. When entering into battle, Samurai warriors shaved the top of their heads—it's thought, to make them more comfortable under the heat of their helmets. Of course, armor was worn in battle, and it was made of steel, wood, or leather and stitched together with intricate lacing and patterns.

This shift in status ultimately caused frustration and conflict within the ranks of the Samurai, who chafed under their inability to participate in merchant activities at a time when this segment of society was rapidly expanding. When combined with a nineteenth-century famine and peasant revolts, this set the stage for the end of the Tokugawa shogunate. Another precipitating factor was the Treaty of Kanagawa, signed between the United States and Japan in 1854. US Navy Commodore Matthew Perry, on behalf of the United States, pressured Japan to reopen to trade and diplomacy. After Japan agreed to sign a treaty, America not only had a trade advantage in the East, but also an eventual consulate on Japanese soil. Finally, in the middle of the nineteenth century, foreigners once again sailed their fleets into Japanese harbors, ending two-and-a-half centuries of seclusion—before the treaty, trade had been allowed only with Chinese and Dutch ships. Shortly thereafter, the Satsuma and Chosu clans, who were vehemently anti-Tokugawa, joined forces under the name of the fourteen-year-old Emperor Meiji to bring down the Tokugawa shogunate.

Known as the Imperial Restoration or the Meiji period, the time between 1868 and 1912 witnessed major changes for the country of

Japan. A parliament was formed that allowed democratic elections, and the emperor appointed a prime minister and cabinet. Confucianism and Buddhism were jettisoned in favor of Shinto, an indigenous polytheistic religion that was thousands of years old and had quietly coexisted with other belief systems throughout the ages.

The feudal system was abolished in 1876, and with it the Samurai class. They were stripped of their stipends and their swords. Yet bushido, or the way of the warrior, later became a term to define the unpublished collections of the Samurai's unspoken honor code, they lived by. The term was not used until the sixteenth century[12]. Its core values were adopted by twentieth-century Japan through the practice of martial arts, which "were not seen only as a way to maintain ancient martial techniques but instead to preserve their traditional value system, bushido, that could be used to nurtured Japan's national spirit."[13]

It was this code of honor—which stood on many centuries of history and had been adopted by generations of Samurai, and even the legendary Yasuke—that young Womble discovered in post-World War II Japan, not the threatening images spread by war propaganda years prior. Womble, under the teachings and guidance of those whose spirit had been enriched by centuries of Samurai knowledge, would come to learn, embrace, and make bushido his own.

---

[12] https://www.britannica.com/topic/Bushido
[13] Jayson Gold-Pambianchi (2019). "Bushido - Way of The Warrior," 14. https://www.researchgate.net/publication/330899938_Bushido_-_Way_of_The_Warrior

INTERLUDE

Dr. John Womble's Decision to Join the Military

"I want to join the US Army," John Womble told his mother one cold morning.

She was standing in the kitchen, fixing breakfast for the family, when she momentarily lifted her eyes off the stove and turned to look at her son. When she met his eyes, she could read only one thing in them: determination. She didn't think twice before saying, "You can't."

"Why not?" he asked, no hint of disappointment in his voice.

She placed her fists on her hips, cocked her head, and said, "Because you're only fifteen years old."

She turned back to the stove to finish cooking, but her son reminded her this conversation was anything but over.

"I can flub my birthday and pretend to be of age," he said.

Her eyes darted back to him.

The doughy smell of freshly baked biscuits began escaping the oven as if inviting the gravy that the woman had been tending to on the stove to hurry up and start thickening.

"You'll just have to sign the consent form," he added, still looking straight into his mother's eyes.

"No, John," she said, unwilling to be the one to give up on this staring contest. Afterall, if her son was headstrong and determined, it was because he took after her. "I won't do it."

"But think about how good it will be for me," he began, making his case. "You're always telling me to stay off the streets, that there's no future there for me."

"Because there isn't," she said, crossing her arms over her chest.

"Then why not let me join the army," he said.

"Because that's no place for a young Black man either," she replied, her tone higher now. "You're good at so many things, John. You're a born athlete. I see something in you when you play basketball or football. But Lord knows you scare me when you leap off the walls and land on sand and dirt pretending to be a paratrooper. I think you're really good at sports and maybe there's something there."

"But—" He tried to say something, but his mother lifted her index finger to let him know she wasn't done making her point yet.

"And if sports are not something that will provide you a safe and solid future, I'm pretty sure you and your younger brother will succeed in your musical career because you two are great with that doo-wop," she said.

She was right. Her two sons had a natural talent for music. Doo-wop, part of the rhythm and blues family, had become popular among Black teenagers after World War II, especially those living in big urban cities like Washington DC, Chicago, and New York. John Womble and his younger brother, who could not afford to buy any musical instruments, trained their vocal cords well enough to be able to produce harmony as they sang a cappella. The genre, which takes inspiration from the church gospel choirs, relies heavily on vocal harmony among members of the group and focuses on themes of love, spirituality, and family values.

"You could dedicate yourself to perfecting your music instead of going to fight for somebody else's cause," she said, turning back to the pot and noticing that the gravy was now ready. She turned the stove off, opened the oven, and took out the biscuits.

Her son's stomach rumbled in hunger.

"No kid from Lincoln Heights is going to become somebody in the music industry, Mom," he replied, looking down his feet.

Lincoln Heights Housing Projects, located in northeast Washington, DC, was a neighborhood made of housing projects and apartment buildings. John Womble and his family called the 325-unit public housing complex their home.

"Says who?" she asked, arching an eyebrow while setting the warm breakfast on the table. "How many times have I told you, John. Just stay focused on what you're passionate about and success will follow."

"Then I want to go in the US Army," he said.

"No!" she insisted.

"But why?" he asked, almost as if pleading.

"Because that's no place for a Black child," she said. "I know who I give to them when I sign those papers for you. I will give them a determined, wholesome, and charismatic young man who loves spending time with friends and family, but I have no idea who they will bring me back when they're done with you."

"I promise you. I won't let them change me," he said, taking a step closer to her.

"What has gotten into you?" she asked, arching her brows. "Up until this morning, you never once mentioned that you had the military anywhere on your radar as your future ambition. Why the sudden change? What happened?"

He looked away and didn't reply. How could he tell her that, the night before, he and his friends had gone to a party and was surprised by how many girls were fanning themselves when a man in uniform walked by. He couldn't tell his mother that this was the moment he decided he wanted to enlist, so he could have the same effect on girls. With the impressionable mind of a teenage boy, he imagined himself wearing the sharp uniform and having girls swoon over him. His mother wouldn't have accepted that as a reason good enough. But at fifteen years old, he thought he knew better.

It took some more convincing, but eventually he managed to have her sign the papers and he was shipped off to US Army Ranger training after getting his General Educational Development diploma (GED). But once there, he quickly recognized that what his mother had warned him about—the military not being a suitable career aspiration for him—was indeed true. The glamourous façade of what it meant to wear a uniform had almost immediately faded away and reality sank in with all of its life-altering consequences. To add insult to injury, he eventually learned that the uniformed guy he admired so much at the party for how popular he was with the ladies, was a complete fraud, not even a real soldier.

He decided he wanted to leave the military and go back home, and he knew just what he needed to do to make the process quick and smooth. He was going to confess to his commander and come clean on how old he really was. He was sure his CO would become enraged, perhaps throw a few choice words at him, and then kick him out as quickly as they let him in. With any luck, he'd be home by dinnertime. It had been so long since he had his mother's delicious food, and he was craving it like a man lost in the desert craves water. He could already hear his mother say, "I told you so" but it didn't matter to him. She was going to be happy to have him back. He could even see if his brother wanted him back in the group—his younger brother *had* become a rather successful rhythm and blues singer. He could go catch up with all of his friends, play ball, and have his old life back. He wouldn't have to think of the army ever again in his life.

But the reaction he received from his commander was not the one he had been hoping for. His CO didn't seem upset. He didn't yell. He didn't throw choice words at him. Instead, he barely looked up at young John Womble standing in front of his desk, confessing to his mistake. All he did was shuffle through a bunch of papers, which occupied most of his desk, and said, "Sorry son, you're in the US Army now."

No, he thought. Confessing to his wrongdoing was his only way out. He was sure this was going to work. But it hadn't.

Sorry son, you're in the US Army now. Those words echoed in his mind like a bad dream. Over and over again.

It was too late. He had given his teenage years away. He had signed up to be part of the military and there was no way out of it. The military was going to decide when it was time for him to return home. He had two options: give up or keep his commitment. Though he now recognized his hasty mistake, John Womble didn't have a single cell in him that wanted to give up. He knew he had to see his commitment through and was going to work hard to make the best and most of it.

He continued his training. Some days were more demanding than others, and with every paycheck, he sent money back home to his mother. Weeks turned into months and months turned into years. Eventually, the time came, and the military decided they no longer needed John Womble. They loaded soldiers on a plane under the pretense of a mission. Shortly afterward they were on the way to the United States. At the time, the army was concerned about soldiers' reactions after being forced to leave the life they had built in

Japan—there had been many cases of suicide among soldiers forced to leave, and the situation deteriorated even more when those soldiers had Japanese girlfriends who also committed suicide. After he was honorably discharged in 1956, he went back home. Though nothing had changed in Lincoln Heights, his mother's prophecy had become true: the young man she had given to the US Army was not the same man the US Army brought back to her. Long gone were the days he thrived surrounded by his friends, as he now wanted to be alone with his large Doberman named Major, an army war dog, whom he brought back from Japan; no more doo-wop for him, for he now stayed silent most of the time, only speaking when absolutely necessary; no more being carefree, for he now was reserved and kept to himself, his friends noticing he moved strangely, with a gait more like a cat than a man. Usually, at Kelly Miller's basketball court they choose team members; everyone wanted Womble on their side as leverage—many players suffered the consequences of roughing him on the court.

But there was also another prophecy of his mother's that turned out to be true. She told him to focus on what he was passionate about and success was sure to follow. During his time in Japan, John Womble had become passionate about martial arts and the Samurai lifestyle. Never before had he been so passionate about something as he was about becoming a true Samurai. Remembering his mother's words, the ones she spoke to him in the kitchen while preparing breakfast, he dedicated himself to what he was passionate about.

Success followed, indeed.

TWO

"To our good and loyal subjects..."[14] Those were the six words chosen by Emperor Hirohito as the opening for his historic speech, which aired at noon, local time, in Japan on August 15, 1945. The night before, while hiding in an underground reading room, he had written, rewritten, and edited his address to the nation until midnight, making sure he didn't use words like "defeat" or "surrender." He knew that his address would reach even the most remote rural prefectures in the nation, where his subjects would be alerted to it by messengers and instructed to gather around the closest local radio. What he hadn't considered, however, was the low and staticky sound quality of said radios, as well as the implications of using the lesser-known classical language instead of colloquial Japanese, the language spoken by most of his subjects. Since his rise to the Chrysanthemum Throne—the throne of the Japanese emperor—two decades prior, this would be the first time he spoke directly to them.

Only a week prior to his historic speech, his country had been on the receiving end of unprecedented destruction, caused by the United

---

[14] "Text of Hirohito's Radio Rescript," *The New York Times*, p. 3. August 15, 1945, Retrieved July 31, 2020, https://www.nytimes.com/1945/08/15/archives/text-of-hirohitos-radio-rescript.html

States when it dropped atomic bombs on Hiroshima and Nagasaki. The tangible climate of uncertainty and fear could no longer be denied: his subjects, now more than ever, were looking to him for guidance, and the forty-four-year-old emperor knew he had to choose his words carefully. There was no better word than "loyal" to describe Japanese people—indeed, they had loyally followed his lead in the Pacific War, which sought to establish the country as a force to be reckoned with and its ultranationalistic ideology as the new way of life. Over the past twenty years, Hirohito had carefully portrayed a rather militaristic image of himself. Wearing only his military uniform—embellished by shiny medals—whenever he appeared in public, he had crafted an intimidating persona, ensuring that his subjects saw him as Japan's commander-in-chief.

Hirohito had encouraged a strong sense of military and ultranationalistic spirit in his people in part by supporting preexisting doctrines of budō—or martial arts—training in schools to "cultivate loyalty, bravery, and heroism in order to bolster the spirit of the nation, while developing principles of devotion and honor."[15] Since the onset of the twentieth century—when Japan had engaged in war, first against Russia (1904–1905) and then again when they began invading China thirty years later—politicians had agreed that teaching martial arts in schools would allow younger generations to learn *reigi*, or traditional budō etiquette. The word budō—武道, the way of the warrior—is comprised of two ideograms (or *kanji* in Japanese); the first ideogram means "war" or "stopping the spear," while the second ideogram means "way" or "path." Combined, the two kanji convey the development of one's spirit and the discipline of the self. By establishing budō training in

---

[15] Quoted in Alexander Bennett, PhD., "A Reconsideration of the Dai-Nippon Butokukai in the Purge of Ultra-nationalism and Militarism in Post-war Japan," Kansai University, 74, accessed August 9, 2020, file:///C:/Users/brune/Downloads/1346_194x_029_06.pdf

schools, younger generations would therefore learn to live by reigi morals and ethics, develop a stronger sense of loyalty toward their nation, and show respect and polite conduct to their peers, elders, and everyone and everything around them. Although it was neither the main focus nor the ultimate goal, the physical benefits of practicing budō in school would eventually produce students who were fit and ready for battle.

Aside from focusing on the importance of budō training, the ultranationalistic spirit of early twentieth-century Japan also celebrated Japanese folklore, from charming tea ceremonies and sentimental songs to dramatic Kabuki theater performances and traditional dances. But the proud identity that the nation had exemplified in recent years had steadily been replaced by the specter of a word that Hirohito, who ruled Japan from 1926 until 1947, made sure wouldn't be part of his speech: defeat. The war-torn country had lost over three million of its own people during World War II, with the Battle of Okinawa being one of the bloodiest. A brutal conflict between the Japanese Imperial Army and the United States Marines and Army, the Battle of Okinawa was the swan song of an emperor whose majestic dream was about to be shattered. For eighty-two days, Hirohito engaged his troops in the futile and devastating effort to stop the Allied Forces from invading the home islands. Hundreds of thousands of Japanese people succumbed to their fate, among them 150,000 Okinawans, with many of them choosing suicide over falling into enemy hands.

Part of the Ryūkyū archipelago, Okinawa was, at the time, its largest and most populated island. The Ryūkyū Kingdom had been a quasi-independent entity up until 1879, when—sixty-six years prior to the Battle of Okinawa—it was annexed by Japan following a forceful military invasion by the Meiji government. Ryūkyū's natives, who, over hundreds of years, had developed their own language, customs, form of government, and traditions, were suddenly forced to adopt a Japanese identity. The Meiji government enforced the teaching of Japanese language and culture in Ryūkyū's schools to eradicate their native lifestyle and languages—students who spoke their native language at school were forced to wear a so-called dialect tag around their neck. Ryūkyūan languages and dialects were also prohibited from being used in official government documents, lands and resources were confiscated and placed under Japanese control, and the practice of the Ryūkyūan faith was forbidden. Rooted in Polynesian beliefs, Ryūkyūan faith was heavily based on venerating ancestors. When during WWII, Hirohito sent his Imperial Army to the island, there were around 300,000 native Okinawans. Within less than three months, half of them would either be killed in action, dead by suicide, or missing.

Witnessing the near disappearance of this minority group was the Twenty-Fourth Infantry Regiment of the US Army, a unit that was mostly made of Black soldiers—also known as Buffalo soldiers—who, because of their firsthand experience with racism and racial segregation, could certainly empathize with a group of people that was forced to fight for a government that considered and treated them as second-class citizens. Active from 1869 to 1951, and then again from 1995 to 2006, the Twenty-Fourth was one of the four all-Black peacetime regiments created in 1866 by an act of congress—although by the beginning of World War II, only two units remained, as the Ninth and Tenth Cavalry Regiments had been disbanded due to the racist policies put forth by then-President Wilson who, after segregating federal officers, decided to exclude Black soldiers from the American Expeditionary Force[16] and chose to have them under French com-

---

[16] The American Expeditionary Force were American soldiers sent to Europe during World War I. However, given the poor training state of most troops, many of them did not make it to the European front until 1918, the year the war ended.

mand during World War I instead. This marked the very first time that American soldiers were left under the command of a foreign nation. The Buffalo soldiers were assigned many different tasks, which also included safeguarding the US mail, protecting settlers, and helping with building infrastructure and roads that would eventually facilitate the US government's westward expansion. Mostly serving the Great Plains region during the many decades of the American Indian Wars, their role was to ensure that the Native Americans would remain within the confines of their government-appointed reservations. It is believed that it was the Numunuu, or Comanche, people who came up with the term "Buffalo soldier."

There are two schools of thought surrounding this word choice: some say that the name generated from the dark and curly hair of the soldiers that resembled the buffalo's fur, while others believe the name came from the mighty bravery and fierceness the soldiers demonstrated in battle. Either way, the Numunuu meant nothing but reverence with the moniker, since the buffalo was a highly respected animal in the Great Plains— it didn't take long for the name to stick and become the official image of the Buffalo soldier regiments. Buffalo soldiers were painfully aware that by enforcing orders on Native Americans who dared to rebel against the confines and restrictions of life on the reservation, they were imposing the systemically racist policies of the US government, the same discriminatory rules that every Black soldier in that regiment was subjected to, both in and outside of the ranks. And when the Twenty-Fourth Infantry Regiment arrived in Okinawa in 1945—under the command of Julian Hearne, a white colonel who had joined the army only four years prior and was now in charge of the all-black unit—they were once again faced with the painful consequences that systemic racism has on marginalized groups. But the proud Buffalo soldiers who, throughout their history, had demonstrated "remarkable courage [. . .] in the face of fierce combat, extreme discrimination in the Army, deadly violence from civilians and repressive Jim Crow laws,"[17] were ready to serve their country and, not too long after their arrival on the island, the Twenty-Fourth Infantry Regiment formally managed and accepted the Japanese surrender of local garrisons.

Less than two months after the end of the battle of Okinawa, and a handful of days after the B-29 Superfortress dropped two atomic bombs on mainland Japan, Hirohito arrived at the Japan Broadcasting Corporation (NHK) and sat in front of the microphone. With tears in his eyes, he remembered the events of the night before, when he had contacted the Allied Forces and offered to surrender, a request that the US Army General Douglas MacArthur, Supreme Commander of the Allied Powers (SCAP), gladly accepted. Then Hirohito took a deep breath and began speaking.

Hirohito's speech was heard across the country and where his troops were stationed overseas. Although it was hard for many to fully comprehend, one sentence in particular stood out among the rest: "We have resolved to pave the way for a grand peace for all the generations to come by enduring the unendurable and suffering what is unsufferable."[18] And with this, Hirohito's dreams of an ultranationalistic identity and political supremacy shattered.

World War II was over.

---

[17] "The Proud Legacy of the Buffalo Soldiers," National Museum of Black History and Culture, Smithsonian, accessed August 10, 2020, https://nmaahc.si.edu/blog-post/proud-legacy-buffalo-soldiers

[18] "Text of Hirohito's Radio Rescript," *The New York Times*, page 3. August 15, 1945, Retrieved 31 July 2020, https://www.nytimes.com/1945/08/15/archives/text-of-hirohitos-radio-rescript.html

When John Womble arrived at Camp Wood in Japan nine years later, the echo of Hirohito's speech still resonated among his people, and the shattered pieces of the emperor's dream were spread across the entire country. The nineteen-year-old paratrooper had joined the United States Army a year prior and had been deployed to Japan with the 187th Airborne Regimental Combat Team—also known as the *Rakkasan*, a Japanese term that means "parachute men" that was used to describe airborne soldiers.

The climate that Womble encountered was certainly tense, just like the one he had left back home and that Black service members—such as the Buffalo soldiers—before him had experienced firsthand. He had joined the United States Armed Forces soon after President Harry Truman had declared that "there shall be equality of treatment and opportunity for all persons in the armed services without regard to race, color, religion, or national origin."[19] Although the president had signed Executive Order 9981 in 1948, formally ending segregation in the US Armed Forces, most senior leadership in the military did not immediately welcome the change and chose instead to ignore it—especially because they considered being in charge of Black soldiers a punishment and something beneath them, so they retaliated against their own troops by making false accusations against them claiming they were unfit to fight and serve. As a result, a young Womble walked right into a *de facto* segregated army, even though *de jure* segregation had formally ended five years prior to his enlistment.

Camp Wood was five miles north of Kumamoto City on the island of Kyushu, the southernmost island in Japan. While it had been home to the Twenty-First Regiment during World War II, it had become an armistice station after the Korean War. The base that

---

[19]   Harry S. Truman, "Executive Order 9981," The White House, https://history.army.mil/html/topics/afam/execorder9981.html

Womble would be stationed at a year after enlisting offered many amenities: a football field that also doubled as a baseball diamond, a chapel, a hospital, and many recreational facilities where soldiers could find a few comforts of home, including sodas and ice cream treats.

The reality outside the base, however, stood in stark contrast to what soldiers enjoyed inside its gates. What Womble witnessed was a country desperately searching for a new identity. Japanese people who didn't have enough food were eating out of garbage cans, women whose loved ones had been killed in action committed suicide, and those who did come home from the war found their country in ruins. The desperation and rage that blanketed Japan at the time could be felt at every corner, as Womble himself witnessed on two occasions—both events were investigated by a court martial and found to be self-defense. According to army records, twenty-year-old John Womble was attacked by another soldier with a custom knife with a hook on the end and severely injured. Investigations showed Womble acted in self-defense. Another instance saw a Japanese male provoke a fight; Womble subdued the man but sustained a cut to his chest. Fortunately, an old Japanese woman dressed the wound and saved his life. After undergoing surgery at the army hospital, Womble noticed that the areas she had treated healed with little to no scarring. Unlike what is shown in the movies, real combat is dirty and unpredictable.

After Hirohito's speech and subsequent surrender to the Allied Forces, Japan had to employ a new set of rules and regulations, which included the prohibition of military education and references to ultranationalistic ideology, set forth by General MacArthur, who quickly alerted Japan's Ministry of Education. This meant that budō training in schools was now prohibited: "In all educational organizations, the teaching of military curriculum must be forbidden. The wearing of student military uniforms must also be forbidden.

Traditional activities like kendo, which foster the fighting spirit, must be abolished, too. Physical education must no longer be linked to 'spiritual education.' You must put more emphasis upon purely physical exercise; games that are not military training, and recreational activities. If instructors wearing military-type uniforms are employed as physical education instructors or engage in sports and physical education activities, they must have their qualifications examined."[20] As a result, budō activities were quickly replaced by group physical training and American sports, such as baseball, that promoted a sense of community as opposed to focusing on developing the self—like martial arts did.

Even though Japan was still searching for its new identity, John Womble could still perceive its old one as he walked around Kumamoto City, including sites like Kumamoto castle. Situated on a hilltop overlooking the city, the castle was fortified by Kato Kiyomasa—a warrior, designer, and distant cousin of Toyotomi Hideyoshi—in 1607 with *musha-gaeshi* stone walls. Musha-gaeshi means warrior repellant—a fitting name since the walls may, at first, seem like an easy climb for an ill-intentioned Samurai or ninja, however they become progressively steeper. Forty-nine turrets, and almost as many gates, greeted the young soldier, who couldn't help but admire Kumamoto's majestic posturing or soak up the elegant yet assertive atmosphere as he approached. The castle—since severely damaged during the 2016 earthquake—was originally stained with a dark color to fight off attacks from wood-damaging insects and to help the walls withstand seasonal change. The Akazu-no-mon (meaning, unopened) is a gate

---

[20]   Quoted in Alexander Bennett, PhD., "A Reconsideration of the Dai-Nippon Butokukai in the Purge of Ultra-nationalism and Militarism in Post-war Japan," Kansai University, 81, accessed August 9, 2020, file:///C:/Users/brune/Downloads/1346_194x_029_06.pdf

located on the east side of the castle and, as its Japanese name suggests, it is a gate that was meant to never be opened so that evil spirits would not be allowed to enter the premises. Kato Kiyomasa chose to also dig one hundred wells on the castle's grounds and plant trees that would provide inhabitants with fuel to burn and nuts to eat. And to ensure that they wouldn't run out of rice, he stuffed the tatami mats that lined the floors with vegetable stalks as opposed to rice straws, which, at the time, were more commonly used.

As Womble looked around, he could indeed see a country that had been forced onto its knees—but he could also sense that its soul was still strong and proud, standing firm on the centuries of Samurai culture that had forged its spirit. It was in 1877, in fact, that one of Japan's most famous Samurai battles occurred on the very grounds Womble was walking on. After hostilities rose between the Emperor Meiji in Tokyo and the Satsuma Domain—part of the Tokugawa Shogunate in Edo from 1602 to 1871—a young Satsuma commander named Saigo Takamori led twenty thousand Samurai to "Tokyo to cleanse the government of corruption. But given his route took him via Kumamoto, now under the control of the emperor and home to the Imperial Japanese Army's largest garrison on Kyushu, [Takamori] knew what had to happen. The castle had to fall."[21] However, the castle did what it had been built to do: protect its people against attackers. Takamori was defeated, and his retreat back to Satsuma was eventually fictionalized in the highly romanticized Hollywood movie, *The Last Samurai*.

Kumamoto City had likewise been home to Miyamoto Musashi, also known by his Buddhist name, Niten Dōraku, and one of

---

[21] Mike MacEacheran, "The Japanese castle that defied history," BBC.com, January 4, 2018, http://www.bbc.com/travel/story/20180103-the-japanese-castle-that-defied-history

Japan's most legendary Samurai. After moving to the city in 1640, Miyamoto—who was known for his unique skills in using two swords at the same time (Niten Ichi) and his undefeated record over sixty duels—spent his last few years in deep meditation, perfecting the art of calligraphy, drinking tea, and writing *Go Rin no Sho* (*Book of Five Rings*), a detailed, philosophical study of the intellectual and behavioral teachings of martial arts.

As he walked around the city, John Womble was accompanied by the spirits of those warriors, surrounded by the shadows of those who had accepted their fate in true Samurai fashion, and inspired by the soul of a fortified castle that had witnessed battles that schoolchildren had studied for generations. It is hardly a surprise that he began to build his legacy as the first African American Samurai right there in Kumamoto City.

INTERLUDE

Dr. John Womble Spends Time in Japan

"Don'tch y'all wanna come to the Texas bar?" a fellow soldier asked John Womble at the end of a long eleven hours on duty that began before the sun woke up and ended well after it had already gone back to sleep. The soldier, who couldn't have been older than nineteen years of age, had a crooked smile that impressionable ladies everywhere said reminded them of Elvis Presley's and deep blue eyes that revealed the naivety of someone who'd never been out of their small town and had never come face to face with the consequences of real life.

"Thank you for the invitation," Womble said politely, hinting at a smile with the corners of his mouth. "I have heard of the Texas bar here on the base, but I would rather spend what little free time I have to soak up the culture of our hosting country."

"Shoot," the blue-eyed soldier said with a laugh and a pronounced southern drawl, waving his hand at Womble as if dismissing his remark. "Why would y'all wanna mix up with them Japs?"

And there it was. The very reason why Womble didn't want to mix up with them at the Texas bar. Racism. He had left racism back in the United States of America, but racism hadn't left him. In fact, it seemed to

34

Womble that racism had enlisted in the military ranks and set up camp in that very Texas bar that this newly arrived soldier was so enamored with. And why wouldn't he? For what Womble had seen and heard about the bar, it was a white man's paradise. A southern white man's paradise, to be precise. The one time Womble did go to the Texas bar was also the last. The moment he entered the room, it felt as though time stood still. There was music playing in the background—country music—but it was as if nobody could hear it anymore. Eyes, which were once glued to large mugs filled with beer, were now staring at the Black man who had just dared to walk into their territory. They were staring at the Other.

The Other, as Womble had always understood, was everything that white people were not. It was a binary opposition, a mindset with historical biases like white and Black, good and bad, right and wrong. It was so ingrained into stories that children instantly assumed the cowboy with the white hat was all that is good. Womble knew that, in the presence of white people, he was the Other. The few times he tried to associate with them he just couldn't understand why they were amicable in private situations but acted as if he was invisible when they were together with the company or in the field. He saw how they became obedient to authority, especially when officers were around—as if they were chameleons. He followed orders but didn't fit the expectations of the in-group, as he was not compliant, nor subservient or pacifist. He was a model soldier and refined.

In order to be John Womble, a young soldier who, against his mother's better judgment, had decided to join the US Army, he knew he couldn't be around white people more than absolutely necessary, or he'd lose his identity because he'd be the Other. And he just wanted to be John Womble.

However, he felt like himself when surrounded by other Others. When he was in the company of Japanese people, he was not the

Other, he was Womble-san. Leaving the often-suffocating confines of the military base to go explore Kumamoto City made Womble feel alive. He enjoyed visiting Japanese bars, where he would drink sake and eat freshly prepared noodle soup, which he always ate with gusto because of their well-balanced broths that carried an intense umami flavor he hadn't eaten anywhere else in the United States—something he knew better not to ever utter in front of his mother.

"I appreciate your inquisitive mind," Womble said to the young soldier. "However, I have also promised our new squadron member here"—he nodded toward another Black soldier who had recently arrived in Japan and stood next to Womble—"to take him with me around town tonight. I shall bear in mind what you said and wish you a fulfilling evening." Before giving his interlocutor a chance to reply with one more racist remark, Womble looked at his new comrade and they both walked away.

"Are there gon' be retaliations?" the new soldier asked, his tone betraying a hint of fear and apprehension that, Womble knew, was absolutely justified given the political climate that afflicted their home country and the systemic racism they had been fighting against their entire—albeit short—life.

Womble, always a man known to talk only when it really mattered, shook his head.

"You sure?" the new soldier asked, his eyebrows arched.

"I'm sure," he reassured him.

After walking out of the base, they made their way toward the bar that had become one of Womble's favorite places to hang out, eat good food, and relax.

"*Konbanwa*, Womble-san," a man standing outside the bar smoking a cigarette greeted him, slightly bowing to his customer.

"Konbanwa, Tanaka-san," Womble said, bowing back.

The man parted the *noren*—the curtain-like fabric dividers usually found in Japanese doorways or windows—indicating they were welcome to enter.

The room was quite dark, but it was filled with people. Almost every table was taken with the exception of two or three. The bar framing the cooking area was completely occupied by patrons. Some of them were Japanese men finally able to relax after a long day at work, but most of them were Korean soldiers who looked like they had seen the worst of humanity, yet still found a reason to attempt to smile. In the back of their minds the trauma of the humiliating defeat by the Chinese and North Korean troops in 1950 and the hubris of General MacArthur left a sense of despair among Allied Forces. The United States of America had also suffered a disastrous defeat by Chinese leader Mao Zedong's masterful execution of SunTzu Bingfa (a compendium of Chinese strategies). Nonetheless, they found moments of solitude and reassurance that they were on the right side.

"What did you two say?" the new soldier asked Womble as he soaked in the atmosphere.

"He greeted me by saying konbanwa, which means 'good evening' in Japanese," Womble explained as he took a seat at what had become his regular table. "Then he called me by my last name and added san to it, which is a way to show respect. It's like saying Mr. Womble."

"And why did he bow?" he asked, sitting at the same table, across from his unofficial tour guide.

"Because it's how Japanese people greet one another," Womble said. "The deeper the bow, the more important the person you're bowing to is."

"I had no idea of Japanese customs," the new soldier said, the look in his eyes matching the truth he had just voiced but revealing a childlike curiosity as well. "How did you learn all of this?"

Before Womble could reply, a young Japanese woman approached the table and asked: *"Minna-san, o-cha o nominasuka?"*

"Hai, o-cha o nomimasu, kudasai," Womble replied.

The young Japanese woman bowed slightly and left.

"I thought we'd start with some tea," Womble said, looking at his young new friend.

"That's what you said to her?" he asked, his eyes wide with stupor.

"Well, no, she first greeted us with Minna-san, which means something like 'everybody.' Although in our case it would be more appropriate to translate it as 'sirs'." Womble waited for that information to sink in, then added: "After the greeting, which as you noticed still carried the san, to show us respect, she asked if we wanted to drink tea, or o-cha as she called it. Cha is tea, but in Japan, they add the honorific letter o before it, to show respect to the tea."

"Th-th-they show respect to the tea?" Womble's friend asked, unsure whether to laugh or take it seriously.

"Indeed," Womble replied with an unwavering expression. "They also show respect to sake, which is why, if you ever wish to order some, be sure to ask for o-sake."

"This is unbelievable," the young man said. "But you haven't answered my question. How do you know all of this?"

Womble leaned forward, as if about to reveal an important secret that only his interlocutor's ears were allowed to receive. Almost as if mimicking Womble's posture, the young man leaned forward as well.

"I care," Womble said, then leaned back in his seat.

The young man stood there and stared at Womble as if to say, "Man, you're a strange cat." Two simple words had been spoken, yet they carried so much weight that the young man needed a moment to fully comprehend their meaning.

"O-cha." The young Japanese woman came back with a steaming

pot of hot tea and two small bowls. She placed them on the table, un-knowingly forcing the young man to finally lean back in his seat too.

"*Arigatou gozaimasu*," Womble said to the woman, bowing ever so slightly. She bowed back and left. "Before you ask me, that meant 'thank you very much'."

The young man was speechless, so he proceeded to take a sip of his tea.

"Whoa!" he said—though it was a borderline yell—when the steaming hot tea touched his lips and the tip of his tongue.

"Yes, tea is hot, as it should be," Womble said. "Also, it's not sweetened, so you might want to prepare your tastebuds for the most bitter green tea they have ever tasted."

The young man blinked twice as if his soul was wondering, "What did I get myself into by agreeing to come here with this man?"

"But you'll get used to it," Womble said, turning the cup three times to the right and taking three small sips. Then, he placed the cup back on the table, turned it three times to the left, and drank at will. It was part of a ceremony he did before drinking his tea as if the hot beverage didn't bother him at all. "If you don't take a shine to it, you just won't come here ever again. If that's what you choose to do, so be it. But for your own safety, I encourage you never to go with those guys to that Texas bar. It's not a place for"—he looked at his friend with such intensity it was as if his stare was speaking directly to his soul—"us."

His friend acknowledged that remark with an agreeing nod. Slowly, he drank the tea without ever commenting on the lack of sugar, and even seemed to do his best not to let his facial expression convey just how bitter it tasted to him. After they had finished the tea, the waitress brought them a bowl of noodle soup each, which they enjoyed in silence. The broth, with its deep flavors, felt like a reassuring embrace that they were in the right place at the right time, doing exactly what they were meant to do.

They didn't feel like the Other. They belonged.

"You're supposed to make noise when you slurp the noodles," Womble instructed him. "It's a way for you to let them know you're enjoying your meal."

"Seriously?" He asked.

Womble nodded.

His friend followed instructions and slurped loudly, eliciting an unexpected smile in his unofficial Japanese culture and lifestyle sensei.

"*Ramen wa oishii desune?*" Womble said.

His friend tilted his head in confusion.

"The noodles are delicious, aren't they?" Womble translated.

"Yeah, so delicious!" he said with a toothy smile.

"Then you have to say, *ramen wa totemo oishii desu,*" Womble instructed him. "It's the literal translation of what you just expressed to me."

He repeated the words, albeit with some difficulty. But Womble repeated it several times so his friend could practice. When the waitress came back to take their empty bowls, Womble's friend repeated the sentence to her, and she kept thanking him and bowing to him for giving her this compliment.

"You made her happy," Womble said.

His friend smiled and looked down at the empty table, almost trying to hide how much he hoped he did make her happy.

"And judging by how often she keeps glancing your way, I'd say you made an impression on her," Womble doubled down.

This time, his friend couldn't hide anything anymore. As if on cue, he looked back and caught her staring at him. She hid her face in her hands, perhaps trying to hide her blushing, forgetting the room was so dark that he couldn't possibly see her cheeks turning from porcelain white to light pink.

"What should I do?" he asked Womble, looking back at him.

"The only thing you can do," Womble said. "Be a man."

"So I should go talk to her?" he asked.

"That's not what I said," Womble specified. "Be a man, whatever that means to you. Be a standup guy, one she'll talk about with a smile on her face, not one that brings her tears and shame."

"This is not telling me anything," he said, lowering his shoulders.

"It's telling you everything you need to know," Womble replied. "But if you can't hear it, then it means you're not ready to hear it."

His friend sighed a heavy sigh.

"It'll come to you when the time is right," Womble reassured him.

Whether he ever understood the meaning of Womble's advice or not, Womble never knew. The young man was sent to Korea a few days after that night, and he never heard of him ever again. Had he been killed in the war? Who knew. Had he ever made his way back to the bar to finally speak to the waitress? Womble surely hoped so.

"Young love is a rare, precious stone," Womble used to say when recalling this episode. "One that only the purest of souls get to experience and truly live."

Though he had no idea how his friend's story ended, he kept his memory alive by sharing stories of the time they met at the bar, how his tastebuds quickly adjusted—and actually began to prefer—the sugarless green tea, how his throat had gotten used to the burning sensation of sake being swallowed down, and how he always slurped as loudly as he could so his young love interest knew he had sincerely enjoyed the meal she had served him.

Womble's first few years in Japan were spent soaking up as much Japanese culture as he possibly could. He felt at home outside the confines of the military base he had been sent to. While in the land of the Rising Sun, he made sure to learn as much conversational Japanese language as he could, making mistakes here and there but working hard to correct them. He attended sumo matches, learned of the strict eating habits these wrestlers had to stick to if they wanted to be able to compete, and also appreciated the company of beautiful Japanese women here and there.

When the military first told him that he was being sent abroad, to Japan, the country seemed so far away, and not just geographically speaking. Never could Womble have ever dreamed of finding home in a country that had absolutely nothing in common with the one where he was born and raised. Yet, he didn't just find home. He found purpose. He found *do*, the way. He found the way forward, the one filled with new goals to accomplish.

In a way, Japan adopted Womble by feeding not only his stomach, but also his spirit. Japan nourished him with a new way to see the world, a new way to treat people, and a new way to appreciate himself. Japan didn't just train his body; it trained his mind first and foremost. In return, Womble dedicated his life to Japan by bringing back with him the countless lessons learned while abroad and sharing them with those wise enough, kind enough, and strong enough to appreciate them.

THREE

"I am not here to educate you on how to kill your brothers in the alleys, how to kill your friends, or how to kill your relatives at home. I'm here to educate you on how to defend yourself mentally, physically, and spiritually." John Womble's voice captured his students' undivided attention as it thundered through the halls of the University of the District of Columbia—formerly Federal City College in Washington, DC—where he taught an elective martial arts class for over thirteen years.[22]

After returning from Japan in 1956, Dr. Womble was honorably discharged from the military.[23] In the hope of going back to Japan, he asked Dr. Chitose for permission to return, but Dr. Chitose felt it was crucial for Dr. Womble to stay in the United States of America and share what he had learned in Japan with those who needed to learn it. Dr. Womble understood that teaching was the most effective way to

---

22 "Federal City College, Washington, district of Columbia, 1968-1978," America's Lost Colleges. https://www.lostcolleges.com/federal-city-college

23 In 1956, Dr. John Womble, like many other military members stationed in Japan, were tricked into getting on a plane assuming it was just another Ranger mission; but halfway across the Pacific Ocean, they realized it was not what they thought. The US military was sending them to Fort Campbell, Kentucky, Eighty-Second Division, to be honorably discharged.

gain mastery of the martial arts and, because of the challenging living conditions in Washington, DC, especially for inner-city youth, he felt it was his mission to help. He systematically surveyed his environment in order to develop scenarios that would allow him to implement the principles he learned in Japan and during his Ranger training. In his elective class at the college, he applied strengths, weaknesses, opportunities, and threats (SWOT) of everyday situations to his teachings.

The college had opened its doors in 1968, one of two—the other being Washington Technical Institute—created after Congress passed the Public Education Act in 1966, which was intended to meet "the needs of the community by directing the resources and knowledge gained through education toward the solution to urban situations." However, after only a decade, Federal City College and Washington Technical Institute were combined with the District of Columbia Teachers College and together formed the University of the District of Columbia.

Between 1968 and 1978, Womble played a pivotal role in the history of the college, a role that only added to the over forty years of selfless and highly dedicated service to the Black community of Washington, DC, a community that, before Womble, had few real role models to look up to, had lost all sense of direction, and could no longer find hope in the future. Womble did not have an easy task to accomplish, and he was highly aware of it. His most complicated obstacle was not poverty and the marginalization of the Black community. Rather, it was its root cause: the pathology of the "dark ghetto," an institutional practice set in place to reinforce the insidious conditioning of slavery after its abolition. But how did this pathology come to be?

To fully understand the reality that Dr. Womble found himself against, it is crucial to recognize the impact that the Great

Migration—which began in 1910, although the majority of African Americans fled in 1940 after the mechanization of cotton farming—had on the demographic and racial structure of the city. The movement, which saw six million African Americans escape the Jim Crow South to look for better life conditions in the North, "was one of the largest and most rapid mass internal movements in history—perhaps the greatest not caused by the immediate threat of execution or starvation. In sheer numbers, it outranks the migration of any other ethnic group—Italians or Irishmen or Jews or Poles—to the United States. For Black people, the migration meant leaving what had always been their economic and social base in America and finding a new one."[24]

Before the Great Migration, 77 percent of Black people lived in the South. However, with the exodus of the Black community to the industrialized North, race and racism became topics of conversation and political debate that reached the ears of those who hadn't been paying too much attention to them. Settling mainly in major cities, including Washington, DC, African Americans soon faced residential segregation that led to the development of racialized urban spaces, which resulted into the creation of the dark ghetto. The ghetto was more than a specific area on the map. It quickly became a sociopolitical and ideological obstacle, as African Americans who lived in residentially segregated communities did not have the same opportunities as their white counterparts. Most insurmountable was the lack of access to quality education, which the *Brown v. Board of Education of Topeka* case didn't really help bring to a more egalitarian platform.

The nation's capital had also become its murder capital, and the situation worsened in 1969, when the FBI reported 83,040 felonies. Crime and violence were not Washington, DC 's only concern though. Washington, DC, was—as it is now—a hub of drug activity

---

[24] Nicholas Lemann, *The Promised Land* (Vintage Books, 1992): 6.

along with notorious gangs of various cultures. The city was also dealing with an opioid crisis that during the 1960s reached epidemic status. Most of the people who fell victim to it were young, working class Black men.

This is the climate that Dr. Womble found when he came back from Japan. It was through his martial arts classes, which he deliberately taught in some of the most deprived areas of the city in order to reach the most at-risk among his fellow citizens—that he extended his helping hand to the youth in a community that would eventually come to think of him as their conscience. Dr. Womble was well aware of the troubled reality that he would face in DC—he was born and raised there—yet he did not shy away from taking charge of the situation. Motivated by the compassion, drive, and love that he had toward the city's underprivileged and at-risk youth, he took it upon himself to become the positive role model they were in desperate need of. As a result, he began serving in as many capacities as he possibly could, first as the manager of several recreation centers while working for the DC Department of Recreation. He was a union officer and an Advisory Neighborhood Commissioner (ANC), testified before the city council about how widespread corruption was in Washington DC, and appeared on radio and TV advocating for the most vulnerable citizens. His emphasis on character building was complicated by Washington, DC's reputation—for being a city that was morally dysfunctional and financially bankrupt. Dr. Womble, however, did not become discouraged by the uphill battle that the nation's capital faced; rather, he asked his students to write, speak, vote, and publicly protest corruption, and he encouraged them to walk the streets to provide community safety. They followed his lead and fought for the city, which remained corrupt but to a lesser degree thanks to his students and their ongoing actions.

Decades later, he even ran for mayor, a clear sign of opposition toward the city's current mayor, Marion S. Barry, who was charged and arrested for perjury, conspiracy to possess cocaine, and drug possession in 1990. Although he was elected mayor for a fourth term in 1995—three years after being released from prison—Barry's inability to aid the city triggered one of its worst financial crises, and eventually led to receivership. During Barry's entire career as the mayor of DC, Womble was outspoken about his disdain for Barry's role in the corrupting of the city and even led the first attempt to recall him.

★ ★ ★

John Womble's commitment to helping people began in 1956 when, back from his deployment to Japan, he started teaching DC's very first martial arts class at the Capitol Recreation Center—thus becoming the first Black man to teach martial arts in the United States. His main purpose was to bring Americans universal concepts, principles, and practices to sustain a healthy community. He offered an alternative to the negative effects of decades of academic practices that lead students to intellectual stagnation. He relied on an inexhaustible reservoir of knowledge acquired at the Kumamoto City School of Samurai, where he graduated from in 1956.

After attending that fateful boxing match in Japan, Womble knew exactly what he wanted: to become a Samurai. His commitment, integrity, and appreciation for martial arts eventually led him to become a student of Dr. Tsuyoshi Chitose, one of the most renowned sensei of his time. Before being able to openly teach martial arts to the US Army, however, Dr. Chitose was forced to mostly teach in secrecy, especially since the martial arts were perceived as being too militarized and partially responsible for the ultranationalistic spirit that had led Japan into a world war.

Born in Naha City, in the Okinawa Prefecture, in 1898, Tsuyoshi Chitose was only seven years old when he began training in karate under Aragaki, a prominent martial arts sensei who is credited with being one of the nineteenth century's most sought-after Tote instructors. Tote, which in Japanese language literally means China (To) Hand (Te)—in Okinawa, martial arts were mostly referred to as 手(te) and were often followed by the name of the art's place of origin, such as Naha-te, To-te—referred to the style taught by Aragaki, which was an agglomeration of Chinese martial arts, hence the name.

Aragaki, who was fluent in Chinese, taught young Dr. Chitose all about Tote, explaining how the style had developed in China one thousand years prior. It was Aragaki's influence that eventually led Dr. Chitose to develop his own style of karate, Chitō-ryū, which means one thousand years, a reference to his instructor's teachings and legacy. Chitō-ryū also included many of the Kata[25], a series of combat and other moves that Dr. Chitose learned under Aragaki, including Shihohai, Niseishi, Seisan, and Sanchin.

It was the blending of Chinese and Japanese martial arts that formed the historical foundation for the martial arts John Womble ultimately taught, Kenpo-Bujutsu. Womble understood how important those roots of martial arts were to Dr. Chitose's teaching philosophy and, as a result, to his own. This might be the very reason that, while teaching at Federal City College, he was one of the most adamant supporters for the addition of a new course titled "Chinese Martial Arts System, History and Philosophy." Doing so also meant bringing the teachings of the Jow Ga style of Kung Fu—developed by Jow Lung, born only eight years before Dr. Chitose. "Since many scholars

---

[25] Kata (型 or 形) means "form" in Japanese language and when used in the martial arts context refers to a series of choreographed movements that the martial artist performs alone.

believe that India and China was the birthplace of Asian martial arts, we feel this would be a fitting tribute to the origin of our cherished arts," Womble said in support of the class.

One of the most important things his students could always count on was his unyielding and uncompromisable dedication to following the physical, mental, and spiritual training he had undergone at the School of Samurai in Kumamoto City. When he himself was a student, Womble studied from 6:00 a.m. to 9:00 p.m. seven days a week even though he was still on active duty—a hazardous task and one that required tremendous balance, which he was able to achieve thanks to a joint project between the US Army and the Japanese Government. The majority of the records of this one-time only event were destroyed along other Army records.[26] The training was extremely physical, but while many succumbed to physical injury or psychological breakdowns, Womble persevered. For example, whenever exhaustion brought on depression and anxiety and left him with little patience, he'd lie on the floor for ten minutes and practice breathing in eight counts to activate his immune system—essentially reestablishing homeostasis within his body.

Aside from the physical training, Womble also had to study the foundations of eastern and western arts and sciences and recapitulate in order to demonstrate understanding. Unlike the traditional western ontological approach. Womble was subjected to rigorous testing that would lead to him remembering, retaining, and retrieving knowledge even under severe stress—a person could be killed or injured in certain situations if they had a delayed response or cognitive dissonance.

---

[26] On July 12, 1973, a disastrous fire at the National Personnel Records Center (NPRC) destroyed approximately 16-18 million Official Military Personnel Files (OMPF). The records affected:

https://www.archives.gov/personnel-records-center/fire-1973

He witnessed students getting maimed, incapacitated, and killed for failing to follow instructions. This type of deep learning is necessary to develop leadership skills in a military environment. After a little over two years and eight thousand hours of study, there were only five students left standing: two Chinese, one Japanese, one white, and one African American—John Womble. Two were delayed in taking the final exam, one because of injury and the other because of indiscretion. Upon graduating at the top of his class, Womble received the Gokai and Jukai Kaidens (fifth and tenth grade Sacred Principles) from his teachers because of his outstanding level of development. In addition, he was given a four-hundred-year-old golden sword—with writing on both sides of the blade or tang—called Katana. At his graduation, he was marked on his upper arms as a testament to his superior level of achievement and development.

As a teacher, Dr. Womble tried his best to help mentally, emotionally, and physically shape his students; contrarily, popular culture depicted the martial arts as pure unadulterated violence. Asian characters were often portrayed in a stereotypical way, denigrated with emasculating voiceovers, and made them sound unintelligent because of their broken English. Movies like *Breakfast at Tiffany's* with Mickey Rooney's infamous yellowface performance as Mr. Yunioshi reinforced stereotypes of Asians as mysterious and deceitful. Meanwhile, popular culture stereotypes of African Americans included lustful, violent, illiterate, or obsequious caricatures, often assuming the form of pimps, muggers, murderers, or bootlickers.

John Womble was aware of these influences and tailored his program accordingly. In order to prepare himself for the mindsets and conditioning of Black people, Dr. Womble studied for a short time at Howard University. He studied the research from noted academicians such as E. Franklin Frazier, Dr. Frances Cress Welsing, Kenneth B.

Clark, and others to better understand the legacy, miseducation, and experiences of his students. He intentionally drew his students from the inner city of DC and other areas of the metropolitan city as well as international students from different parts of the world. His classes were open to the entire world without favoritism. In addition, there were law enforcement officers and military service members studying martial arts to enhance their training.

In the 1970s, several groups used martial arts and eastern philosophies to entice people to adapt radical doctrines—using martial arts to impart violence instead of sticking to its core beliefs and teachings. Washington, DC, alone attracted various radical organizations, esoteric groups, cults, and fads. Therefore, Womble initially and intentionally taught Kenpo-karate-do. The term "do" means "way" and applies to a method of teaching that disengages the tactical approach of the more dangerous parent arts (Bujutsu or Military Arts/Sciences). For example, judo is meant to teach character and is derived from Jujutsu. The pioneer of judo was Dr. Jigaro Kanō, an educator who created judo to improve the mental and physical health of his students. He regarded judo as an art and a science and a way (do) of life. Jujutsu—the parent of judo—is a form of combat that both maximizes the body as a weapon and endorses the use of actual weapons in life and death situations. Simply put, the addition of jutsu implies the deliberate application of martial arts designed for the battlefield or defense against deadly threats. The collective types of martial arts are called Bujutsu and they often lead to death of one or both contestants. Most of what we know as martial arts in North America falls under the category of do or sport.

The do were crafted from jutsu—or in Chinese "Wushu"—in the mid-1900s with the original intention of paving the way to the resulting arts. For example, Aikido, Iaido (graduated training from bokken, to blunted blade, to shinken), Judo, Karate-Do, and Kendo are designed to practice without the high risks or consequences of the more dangerous arts. Many of the Ko-ryu (classical traditions) or old systems use live weapons and strategic attacks meant to maim, incapacitate, or kill. The idea of Kata, or forms, was practiced by judo practitioners. Later, the concept of dans or ranking and kata transferred to karate-jutsu. Before, practicing bouts between jujutsu practitioners could be fatal. As for the importance of teaching character, the war history of America, China, India, Japan, and Korea shows the importance of emphasizing temperament as a perquisite for training martial artist or military science experts. On the other hand, a disciplined military or martial arts doctrine can eliminate unnecessary conflict that may escalate into war. Records of war crime trials after World War II emphasize the consequences of abuse of power driven by martial or military zealots in the East and West—Japan regulates and respects the benefits and disbenefits of martial arts and sports, and the country has one of the lowest crime rates of any industrialized nation.

Of all the various Chinese, Japanese, and Korean styles he studied, John Womble's primary system was Japanese Kenpo. Notably, Masters Chitose as well as Funakoshi wrote books titled *Kenpo Karate-Do* and *Ryukyu Kenpo Karate* respectively. Furthermore, Dr. Chitose assisted Master Funakoshi in developing *Kenpo Karate Do*. John Womble also taught Kenjutsu, Akijujutsu, and Iai-Jutsu to Bugui-sha or exponents of Bujutsu. He learned the Katori Shinto Ryu system in the School of Samurai. The foundation of his knowledge is encapsulated in a framework only known to his twelve masters. The Kenpo forms or patterns of movements are a blend of measures designed to increase mobility and agility while improving the framework for additional systems. Essentially, tactical training. Systems refers to the term Bujutsu, or the fifty-two arts of the Samurai.

Kenpo is the original name for Okinawan martial arts commonly referred to as karate. The historical origins are associated with a Shaolin monk from the central temple in China. As an expatriate living in Japan Chin Gempin (or Genpin) shared his art (Go-Shin-Jutsu) with three ronins or masterless Samurai. Over time, the original system took on several names. The masters shared their experiences—it was this blending of Go Shin Jutsu and Bujutsu that formed the posterity (Kenpo-Bujutsu.). Simply put, the Japanese Kenpo Bujutsu system is the product of vetting of the masters or gate keepers over hundreds of years. Each instructor is expected to be better than his sensei, as Kenpo masters strive for continuous improvement.

Womble translated Kenpo as the Invisible Sword or Ken, meaning Sword and Po referring to Ninpo (Art of Ninjutsu or Intelligence). It is important to note that numerous changes were made to the names of Okinawan martial arts over time and when Japan became more nationalistic, the Kempo system was modified to conform with the patterns of Japanese martial arts. Prior to its restructuring, the art had more Chinese influences. The Japanese adapted a direct approach to the fight or straight line, while Chinese systems with exceptions were mostly circular or, in the case of warfare arrays, each with its strengths and weaknesses. As a result, learning and training in martial arts in Japan and China was challenging and something a person with no experience would do. As for Womble's students, learning about a culture they previously had little access to, had an empowering impact on them, especially those who were treated as inferior. The outcomes were not always positive. Unfortunately, commercialization of martial arts has brought about dangerous consequences.

Today, the distortion of martial sports causes significant damage to young children in the United States according to the American Pediatric Association. Simply put, the purpose of martial arts is to develop character—especially when educating children. For every karate kid there are ten karate bullies, because when children are trained to attack in martial sports, often they become contentious and egotistical as opposed to exemplary students. The distortions go contrary to the intentions of the old masters. Specifically, uncontrolled fighting contests often encourage sadistic behavior—and regularly bleeds over to public and private schools and the community and can pave the way to criminal behavior. Unfortunately, the idea of character building was the last thing most thought of when it came to understanding the intent of the pioneers of martial arts—there's little profit in taking the time to emphasize character building. Instead, many contemporary schools of martial arts prioritize aggression as opposed to self-defense, selling belts, and emphasizing tournaments for instant profit.

The very concept of *dōjō* (道場), which in Japanese means "a place of the way" and comes from the Sanskrit word *Bodhimanda* (where Buddha achieved enlightenment), has been altered by western standards. While in the United States of America the dōjō is conceived as a gym or a place to train physically in martial arts, in Japan it is a place for mental training, not just physical. Given that Samurai in Japan used to train outdoors and not in enclosed spaces, the dōjō was mainly a place to meditate and used for religious purposes back in the Nara period (710–784 CE). As such, the dōjō in Japan has always been regarded as a place where one goes to achieve spiritual and mental excellence, as well as physical. Thus, Japanese Samurai follow a strict, fundamental dōjō etiquette. People entering and exiting must first do a standing bow. Facing the dōjō with knees straight and together, the martial artist bows gently to the dōjō to show it respect and commit to the discipline it expects of the student. Once inside the dōjō, the student must sit in a traditional Japanese way called *seiza*, where the student kneels with both legs folded underneath the buttocks, ankles turned outward, and hands resting on their thighs. *Makuso*, which stands for silent meditation, is enforced in Japanese dōjō because it is believed that it cleanses the student's mind of past and future preoccupations, thus giving way to harnessing the mind and understanding on a much deeper level what the student can do to make a difference in the world. Each repetition of movements, sounds, and setting carries forward the audiovisual literature of the history of martial arts—as living suttas (sutra). After all, the character of a nation is defined by the actions of its citizens—might doesn't make right. History shows that in the best of times the military restores peace and promotes culture both in the home country and abroad. There is civil service and military service; in order to balance society, the two must be understood and regulated. Civilians must be fit to serve if necessary (this was the original intent of sports and contest since the gladiators were admired for their character as well as martial prowess).

Originally, tournaments were pioneered by Dr. Chitose in Canada in order to give martial arts practitioners the opportunity to test themselves in a controlled environment. Unfortunately, when tournaments became popular and profitable, the competitive mindsets created an environment of violence. Former Master Conde, known for sponsoring tournaments in Maryland, eventually had to hire armed security to maintain order. Several martial sports businesses groom students to be aggressive with slogans such as "Fight hard" while outside the dōjō some students were promoting illegal fighting (Fight clubs), provoking attacks in bars, and committing crimes in neighborhoods using ninja practices, thus emphasizing the violent aspect of martial arts over character development. This happened during the time John Womble taught and is perhaps why he was never widely known as others—because he refused to exploit martial arts. Even today it's a struggle to interest people in studying traditional martial arts because of the belief that aggression is the purpose of karate. To the contrary, most traditional teachers emphasize loyalty and justice or respect for laws and beliefs and principles of cultures that influenced their styles and systems. The understanding is further complicated by various conflicting theories about the origin of styles and systems of martial arts. One thing's for sure: Dr. Jigorō Kanō, Gichin Funakoshi, and Dr. Chitose were unified in teaching that martial arts is for character building.

★   ★   ★

John Womble's dōjō was on Sixteenth and Q Street NW in downtown DC, and offered, among many other benefits, a place to find peace to many Vietnam veterans, who returned feeling ignored, trivialized, and shunned, and who suffered debilitating anxiety now known as Post Traumatic Stress Disorder (PTSD). These veterans respected John Womble both because he, too, had served in the military and because he was a fighter in and out of the dōjō, especially for causes important to veterans.

However, not everybody showed such respect toward Womble (though many still did, both on campus and in the streets). Unfortunately, there were attempts to radicalize students and soon Womble found himself in the position of having to ensure his students' safety, along with teaching them how to be productive citizens. One of the most frightening attempts occurred in Bethesda, Maryland, in the 1980s, where an Iranian man was assassinated. The investigation revealed that the suspects were recruited from federal city college, and some of them studied martial arts. Some of Womble's students knew a few of them well, as they were close associates. The suspects were convicted, and records show the order to assassinate came from Ayatollah Khomeini.[27] Over the years, they tried to lure Womble's students into local cults in order to engage in activity that could lead to criminal prosecution. Aggressive recruitment prompted a special law enforcement task force formed by the FBI and local law enforcers to infiltrate and investigate some of these activities. That time, the 1970s and '80s, was a tough period in American history because people were protesting the Vietnam war and military drafts and advocating for more rights for all African Americans, and other causes such as the legalization of recreational drugs. Even peaceful demonstrators were attacked by the police, fired upon by the national guard, like the college students who were killed at Kent State.[28] Other campuses were rife with hype and became recruitment grounds for legitimate and fringe religious and radical groups. Some groups were under surveillance by law enforcement because of fears that they would spark violence, and Womble's students possessed some of the same martial skills that radical groups used to their advantage to bully their members into submission. Womble used his reputation and gravitas to influence his students to make smart decisions in order to keep them safe. He kept them engaged in healthy activities and encouraged conversation to keep students occupied as well as out of proximity so they would be safe.

---

[27] https://casetext.com/case/butler-v-united-states-46 Al Fletcher Hunter, an accomplice who testified for the government after a grant of immunity, came to know Belfield through martial arts training and first heard of the assassination plan in mid-June 1980, when Belfield showed him pictures of Ali Akbar Tabatabai and other opponents of the Ayatollah Khomeini.

[28] Kent State Shooting - Causes, Facts & Aftermath - HISTORY
Four Kent State University students were killed and nine were injured on May 4, 1970, when members of the Ohio National Guard opened fire on a crowd gathered to protest the Vietnam War. The tragedy was a watershed moment for a nation divided by the conflict in Southeast Asia.

Still, some of his students were trapped in neighborhoods where deviant behavior was the norm. It was no secret that children were drinking water contaminated with lead and suffering from malnutrition, conditions similar to those Womble witnessed in postwar Japan. Nevertheless, he kept applying lessons learned from his primary sensei and, when Dr. Chitose passed away in 1984, he became a masterless Samurai (ronin).

Dr. Womble traveled to Japan in 1960s with his first-generation students to participate in a martial arts event and visited his masters. Then, a decade later, his masters came to DC to see what he had accomplished. They witnessed Womble's students performing on the Washington, DC, monument grounds. Afterward, the masters impressed by the gestures and execution of precise movements, they bowed, showing him the highest respect for his accomplishments. It was the students body language that spoke—de facto proof that he was able to build on previous knowledge and outrival. They understood the overwhelming challenges Womble overcame to transform his students—such as Tyrone Aiken, who was able to overcome the violent realities he faced in Washington, DC, and eventually became a physical science technician—into productive citizens.

Womble always made sure to continually monitor their development, a task that many—Dr. Womble taught hundreds of students over forty years—might find unfathomable. It required the application of all the knowledge, wisdom, and strength he could muster. He understood that in the East, the teacher was responsible for the actions of their students. Unfortunately, there were students who went rogue and exploited martial arts—some ended up in court and charged with abuse of students due to unlawful training in the legal sense. In some cases, he revoked licenses. Despite the setbacks, he continually assessed his teaching methods, filtering out bad apples and replacing outdated teaching theories that put too much emphasis on doing bodily damage to their competitors with more progressive ones. Dr. Womble was also firm in his belief that encouraging students to learn the Chinese, Japanese, and Korean terms commonly used in martial arts was ludicrous if they did not have a comprehensive grasp of their native language. He would often explain what Japanese terms meant in context but felt that teaching foreign words without offering a more thorough explanation of the context where the word was used was preposterous. As for the physical training, he often held classes out-doors in public parks so that people who walked by could both see his students perform and witness their ability to remain undistracted by crowds, traffic, and weather. Womble was critical and demanded the highest intellectual and physical standards from his students, holding them to the same standards his Japanese teachers had required of him. As did his masters, he practiced marking (inserting signature moves) in his katas and left trapdoors in techniques in order to identify and neutralize corruptors. However, he soon discovered that some of his former students were counterfeiting his credentials and labeling them-selves ninja, Samurai, and karate masters and teaching martial arts to other people. Given that Dr. Womble's reputation as a Samurai was renowned throughout the nation's capital—and elsewhere—some of his former students went as far as exploiting Womble's name in order to raise their profits. This realization hurt Womble's feelings—and reputation—because these students only cared about making money as opposed to preserving the sacred glory of Samurai core values. As a result, Womble became much more guarded and selective when it came to choosing whom he was going to teach. Over the course of forty years, Womble educated three generations of students, but as his reputation grew, so did envy and jealousy among local teachers—some resorted to spreading misinformation, like claiming he was

Asian and not African American; others traveled to Japan in attempts to unearth information to expose him as a fraud.

Rumors even spread that Womble was just a lecturer and didn't compete in tournaments because he was afraid to fight. It was during this time that something odd happened at Womble's dōjō.

"What has happened here?" Dr. Womble said as he walked in the dōjō one Saturday. His pace steady and slow, he kept looking down at the floor, now maculated with dark red spots. He kneeled to take a closer look, then quickly looked up at his students and said, "Why is there blood on the floor?"

His students didn't reply. Instead, chuckles echoed throughout the room.

"Is there something I should know?" he asked, standing back up and looking at each and every one of his students.

His gaze had power. It evoked respect and called for everyone's attention.

"There is, sensei," a white belt student said, taking a step toward Dr. Womble.

The sensei didn't say anything. The silence he offered was enough to ask the student to elaborate on his statement. So, the student began explaining what had happened.

"Lately, when you have been away from the dōjō, other schools in the area have been sending their best fighters here to intimidate us and challenge us with the excuse of seeking free sparring practice," the student said, his voice calm and devoid of any stress of agitation. "We found out that they had a tendency to conceal their ranks, pretending to be at our same level when in reality they were black belts."

Dr. Womble's stoic expression did not reveal any emotion. He listened intently and the student continued.

"They thought we were unskilled fighters because they saw us wearing a white belt," the student said, prompting a giggle from the other students who were trying hard not to burst out laughing. "I guess they didn't know that when we joined your dōjō you made us relinquish our previous ranks, even if some of us had achieved black belt level in sport karate."

Dr. Womble's expression was still unreadable, but he thundered: "Which is not the same as traditional martial arts, as you know. A black belt in sport karate is the equivalent of a white belt in Kenpo-Bujutsu, which is what I teach."

The students nodded.

"Does the blood mean that you all welcomed them as sheep in a wolf's den?" Dr. Womble asked.

The students nodded once again, their eyes beaming with pride and the corners of their mouths curling upward as they recalled what led to the blood stains.

"As you know, I don't condone violence of any kind," Dr. Womble said, now walking toward his students, never losing eye contact with them, something that kept them at attention and on their toes because they didn't know if he was going to be upset with them or the students coming from other schools or both. And if he was upset, the students didn't know what the consequences were going to be.

"I have told you more than once," Dr. Womble said, standing in front of them, "traditional martial arts training encourages making the body invincible first, before engaging in combat. That's why I have noticeable physical changes, especially in my hands and feet. My thumbs were broken in the School of Samurai in Japan and were reset, so they became weapons designed to penetrate vulnerable parts of my opponent's body. My feet were hardened to break bones. I've showed you time and time again that my fist can break cinder blocks."

His students stayed quiet, recalling the times during which they witnessed incredible strength on their sensei's part, marveling at his understanding and awareness of his own body.

"However, just because this is something I can do, it doesn't mean I am going to take advantage of it and seek violence," he said. "What we do here is we encourage the body to become invincible, but we ready the mind to be unbreakable. So, who wants to fight now?"

None of his students came forward.

"Come on, I want each and every one of you to attack me, one at a time." He turned his head toward the farthest student from him, and that was enough for the selected individual to understand he had to go first.

He walked at the center of the dōjō and attacked his sensei, who acted in defense. The student was surprised because he assumed Dr. Womble would go on the offensive. Dr. Womble demonstrated just how dangerous it was to attack when he was able to anticipate the student's every move and that high kicks were especially dangerous because they exposed vital parts of the body. Later, when the training ended, the students revealed that hitting and kicking their sensei was like impacting a boulder.

"You know that martial sports counter the risks by forbidding kicks to the groin and punches to the face, eyes, and throat," he told his students after they recovered from the training. "Just remember that such rules do not apply on the street and thus it is unwise to practice tournament fighting."

The students nodded in agreement.

"But sensei," one of them said, "these students who came here for free spar practice said their own sensei believe you are just a talker, not a doer. Can't we just start competing with them like the other schools do so they don't consider us beneath them?"

Dr. Womble didn't reply right away. He thought about it, and after a few minutes of silence, said, "We will put these rumors to rest once and for all before they result in damaging effects to your self-confidence, as I don't want idle chatter to shake the foundation of what you have been learning." He paused for a moment, then added, "I will take part in the tournament. On one condition only."

His students waited for him to explain further.

"We are going to keep only one trophy," he said, highlighting the message by raising his index finger. "Because our sense of self-worth goes beyond a trophy. Do we all agree?"

The students exchanged a look and then turned toward their sensei, offering him a smile that was proof enough for Dr. Womble that he had their support.

Following this conversation, he made good on his promise and entered several tournaments. He fought and won, and his reputation spread from coast to coast.

At one event featuring celebrities and local fighters from the East and West Coast martial sports organizations, he gained attention as a formidable combatant. A *Black Belt Magazine* article described the event and further amplified Womble's abilities. However, he became seriously concerned about the glaring difference in the way some westerners were corrupting the martial arts to create choreographed moves that had no practical benefits. More specifically, his students were hurting and, in some cases, crippling opponents. He was determined to find out the reasons for the consequences and immersed himself in the study of the leading Japanese, Korean, and Chinese systems to find answers. His achievements in these systems were accomplished by learning from Masters Ki Whang Kim, Sifu Dean Chin, and Francisco Conde, who were close friends as well as respected associates. In fact, the signature Sword Kata for the Japanese Kenpo

Bujutsu.Ryu (JKBR), USA Inc., was created by Womble in honor of Master Francisco Conde. The Kata (Lágrimas), or Thing of Tears, has caused judges and some students to become mesmerized and tear up and pass out. After researching the way martial sports was being taught in the USA during the 1970s, he discovered fatal flaws. He learned that many popular martial sport systems were modified and thus left openings in their students' defenses leading to fatal outcomes.

To make sure he taught the martial arts he learned while in Japan, he immersed his students in Zen meditation (Zazen, Renzai style Zen) and Shiatsu, and macrobiotic principles. "You must learn to cure before learning how to kill," he would often say. The third generation were rigorously trained and educated in greater detail about the arts of the Samurai (Bujutsu). They were the closest he came to reproducing the type of experience he had in the School of Samurai. Notably, much of the training in the School of Samurai was impossible to accomplish in the US, but he adapted his teaching methods to the environment and the legacy, education, and personalities of his students. He continually reminded them of his legacy.

Educated, equipped, and enriched with centuries and centuries-worth of martial arts philosophy and teachings, John Womble made his way back to his home in Washington, DC, where he committed his life to share his knowledge with his people. "If you cannot communicate with people, how can you defend your rights?" His voice thundered once again through the halls of Federal City College. "If you cannot spell, if you cannot write, then you do not know how to project a point. I will set an example for you by speaking correctly, by being persuasive in my speaking, by being logical in my speaking, and by being just in my disposition here. Because that is what I call self-defense. If you think you came here just to learn how to knock your brothers and sisters down, you've got another boat coming.

That is not all this class is about. That part of the class is number ten. Before you get to number ten, you've got to first learn how to develop character."

And following the same doctrines he learned from Dr. Chitose and his other masters, help them develop character he did.

INTERLUDE

John Womble in the Korean War

Sitting in a theater on a Friday evening, waiting for the Kabuki performance to begin, John Womble couldn't help but wonder where he would be spending his next Friday night. It had only been a few hours since he received orders to go to Korea, and he was scheduled to be deployed in a few days. Though he had been practicing meditation to quiet the mind, the heart of a young man who had recently left his mother's safe household still beat faster when images of what a real war fight would look like flashed before his eyes. It didn't help that he had heard all kinds of horror stories coming from the war front. Tales of badly injured comrades at the hands of North Korean and Chinese fighters, tangled with stories of prisoners of war being tortured in the most brutal and inhumane ways, made even the strongest man feel a jolt of fear rush through his body.

Will I become a prisoner of war? He thought to himself. *Will I go missing in action? Will my mother survive the news if I were to die here?*

But for now, the magnitude and finality of what being a prisoner of war or missing in action could potentially mean didn't have a chance to form, fortunately, because Japanese performers started walking on stage to begin their theatrical recital, accompanied by the melody of *taiko*, a large wooden drum typically played in Kabuki shows. The actors, all men, were dressed as Samurai or in colorful, elegant kimono—long robes of different colors, decorated with flowers, cranes, or other animals. John Womble had always been fascinated by kimono, and he had seen many women walk around the streets of Kumamoto City wearing the traditional Japanese attire. Curious, he had asked a Japanese woman he had become friends with what the details on the kimono symbolized, a question she was pleased to answer with a detailed description.

"Every kimono is different," she said. "Depending on a woman's age, marital status, what season it is, what type of ceremony she's attending, what time of day it is, she'll wear a different kimono. For example, a young woman who is not married yet can wear a light pink kimono with longer sleeves and embroidered with *sakura*, cherry blossoms, during spring. However, if it were winter, she couldn't wear a kimono decorated with sakura because they don't bloom in that season."

"Can men wear the same fashion kimono?" Womble asked.

"Of course," the woman replied. "But it has to be more somber and in darker colors. You won't find men's kimono with flower decorations, for example. However, if you pay attention to the back of the jacket, right by the shoulders you'll notice that they have their family crest. This is very important because it shows which family they belong to, and with family, comes social status."

"So why do men wear women's kimono when they perform in Kabuki?" he asked. A big fan of Kabuki, Womble attended as many shows as possible while in Japan, and one of the first things he had noticed was that there were no female actors, just men.

"Because they play the role of women," she explained.

"Why wouldn't women play their own roles?" he asked, ever the inquisitive mind.

"*Onna Kabuki*, meaning women's Kabuki, was banned in the mid-1600s being considered too provocatory, and as a result, too dangerous for public morality," she said. "However, female roles in Kabuki were not erased, which is why men began playing both female and male roles in their theater performances and why you see men wearing women's kimono on stage."

They banned women's Kabuki, and now they are trying to be secretive about playing Kabuki in general, Womble thought as he watched the actors on stage take their places and get ready to begin the performance. He had learned that, after World War II, Japan was in a state of rebranding, so to speak, and they did all they could to stay clear of what Japan and Japanese culture were all about before the country's defeat on the world stage.

Kabuki, along with Samurai schools, had fallen prey to the rebranding. However, for Kabuki, this wasn't the first time it happened. In the late 1800s, the classic Japanese theater had already been influenced by western theater after Japanese scholars traveled outside of the country and brought back with them knowledge acquired abroad. Even the name Kabuki had changed spelling, as it went from 歌舞妓 (which meant song, dance, and prostitute) to 歌舞伎 (meaning song, dance, and skill). This slight change in name bestowed upon Kabuki a sense of intellectuality and morality, thus elevating its educational purpose.

If only American media culture changed its ways too, John Womble thought as he sat in the theater. He was mainly referring to the way in which white America promoted and projected racism through radio shows and movies like *Amos and Andy* and *The Birth of a Nation*, which portrayed Black people as unintelligent, sexually aggressive toward white women, or either clowns or crooks. Meanwhile, the Ku Klux Klan was portrayed as heroic protectors of freedom and womanhood. Womble was aware that these racist representations did not remain within American borders either because he had often overheard white American soldiers tell Japanese women that Black men had tails.

Still, I don't understand why Japanese people are forcing themselves to assimilate into western culture, Womble couldn't help but wonder. *Don't they fear losing the very fabric of what makes Japan and its culture unique?* Fleeting thoughts kept his mind too busy for his liking and he realized he had been so absorbed by his overactive brain (what Buddhist monks refer to as monkey mind) that he hadn't even noticed one of the actors had begun to sing his opening song.

Many of his fellow soldiers had asked him why he bothered attending Kabuki performances when he couldn't understand a single word of what they said (he had started to learn colloquial Japanese language but was far from being fluent enough to actually understand words in a Kabuki performance). His presence alone at Kabuki shows raised quite a few eyebrows from the few white Americans who wondered why a young Black soldier was such an enthusiastic observer (attending a Kabuki performance was considered a sign of intellectuality, of being worldly, two qualities that most white Americans at the time did not associate with Black Americans). Though Womble had always been quick to reply, "because I want to learn more about this country and its culture," he now asked himself the same question.

Why am I here every time I can, even though I cannot understand what they're saying? The answer was right in front of his eyes. Sure, Japan was in a deep state of rebranding, but its people were doing their best to hold on to their culture and identity. They defied government orders that banned Kabuki and Samurai training, along with anything else the West considered too feudal, and as such, a threat to the Allied

Forces. Every actor and musician on that stage was there to say, "We are still here!" and "We will not deny our cultural identity because you're scared of it."

Shivers rushed down Womble's spine when he came to that realization. As a young Black man, he knew all too well what growing up in a society that was scared of what was perceived as different felt like. He knew there were certain things, attitudes, and words he could only say around other Black Americans if he wanted to stay safe. Racial segregation and systemic corruption in the United States of America were at the forefront of why Womble could empathize with Japanese people.

Perhaps that's why I enjoy coming to Kabuki, he thought. *It's my way of supporting their mission in how they stay true to their cultural identity and how they strive to survive in a world that keeps telling them they can no longer be who they truly are.*

True, he couldn't understand everything the actors said, but that didn't matter, because he could *feel* the performance. Through music and body language, John Womble's emotions were aroused but very much involved in what he witnessed on stage. Slowly, he realized that everything people do or say speaks of their thoughts and culture. In every performance he attended, the galloping rhythm of the drums would eventually match his heartbeat, the melody of the *shamisen* (a three-stringed musical instrument with a long neck and a body or hide made of either dog or cat skin) would tug at his heartstrings and make him feel nostalgic, and the vibrant sounds of *fue,* a Japanese bamboo flute, would breathe life into him.

Bamboo.

Never before had that word infused such fear in him. But after receiving orders that morning to go to Korea, bamboo now encapsulated a terrifying imagery. No longer just a symbol of flexibility, growth, and strength; bamboo now represented a weapon, one that North Korean and Chinese fighters had used against American soldiers. Many of the stories he overheard being whispered by other scared soldiers around the base involved a sharpened bamboo stick taken to a really high temperature and used to poke and burn holes in American soldiers when they were captured. Then reality crept in. "The worst part is that these wounds did not even kill them, man," an American soldier said to a comrade while recounting the story that John Womble overheard. "They got poked just for torture, for pure torture."

"How did they get captured though?" the other soldier asked.

"Some say they were captured the moment they made their way down from the airplane," he said. "Them North Koreans and Chinese were waiting for 'em to get closer to the ground, and when they did, they threw bamboo spears at 'em. Man, I'm telling you, they didn't even see that coming because them North Korean and Chinese fighters were hiding in the jungle or in the open fields when the Americans jumped out of the airplane. Can you believe it? You jump off the plane and get impaled by one of them hot bamboo sticks like you're pork on a skewer. That's gotta be just about one of the worst things you could feel, I reckon."

"Man, if I gotta be tortured and then killed, I'd rather have them shoot me right in the head so I won't have to go through hell first," the soldier said. "I ain't jumping off no damn plane, I tell ya."

"It's not just the plane though," he explained. "I heard that a couple of years ago, Americans were ambushed while in a truck convoy by them North Koreans. When they found their bodies, they had over twenty stab wounds, man, all of them from 'em hot bamboo sticks. They knew where to hit 'em, too, because these poor souls were left to bleed to death."

After hearing that, Womble felt as though the air around him had gotten much thicker and almost impossible to breathe. The reality of what could happen to him explained right there for his ears to listen to and his heart to fear.

Is this the fate that awaits me there? He thought to himself.

He had heard of many other tragedies that American soldiers suffered at the hands of the North Korean and Chinese fighters, but for some reason it was the bamboo spears that terrified him the most. Even the Taejon massacre—where sixty American soldiers were made prisoners of war, forced to sit in shallow ditches with their hands bound, and shot and killed at point-blank range by North Koreans with US M1 rifles—didn't frighten him as much.

Maybe that young cat was right, John Womble thought. *Maybe if it's written that my life has to end in Korea, I'd rather be shot at point blank range than be tortured with bamboo sticks or like those guys in the Sunchon Tunnel massacre.*

He was referring to the 138 US soldiers who had been captured by North Koreans as they approached Pyongyang. Wounded, starved, and dehydrated, the prisoners were taken to the Sunchon Tunnel where, after being exposed to the elements of a cold Korean fall, were shot to death.

Many other stories flashed across Womble's mind, which had been so busy recalling these unspeakable atrocities of war, that he had not even realized the Kabuki performance was over. Only when he saw most attendees leave the premises, did he come back to the present and become aware that he had allowed his mind to do the one thing he knew could actually get him killed: panic.

Difficulties strengthen the mind as labor does the body, he reminded himself of something he had heard often from martial artists since he moved to Japan. His upcoming deployment to Korea certainly had the potential to challenge him with many difficulties; but he had the power to control his mind and not let difficulties translate into panic, which was the only way difficulties would turn into defeat.

He got up and slowly walked out of the theater, but not without glancing back at the stage where the actors were still standing. Tall, proud, and strong in their belief that they had accomplished their mission once again: prove to fellow Japanese people, their government, and perhaps even the world, that they were not going to give up their identity and give in to outside pressure.

Nor will I give up on my purpose and give in to fear, Womble thought as he returned to the base.

A few days later, he got on a military airplane and was taken to North Korea. When he was told to jump—after all the white soldiers had jumped—he learned that his nightmare had come true: hot bamboo sticks were being thrown at American soldiers as they made their descent. Parachutes had been punctured and soldiers had been wounded. The chutes lay spread out like blossoms—an unwritten eulogy. Still, he jumped.

But how that part of the story ends will forever remain a mystery. For John Womble never fully spoke about the time he spent in Korea, preferring instead to recall the many times he attended Kabuki performances and how the Japanese people, under pressure to assimilate, maintained their cultural identity alive one drumbeat, string, and song at a time.

FOUR

It was September 17, 1987, in the mountains of West Virginia during one of many fishing trips that mondo—dialogues—occurred between Dr. Womble and one of his students. Bugeisha (meaning exponent of Bujutsu) Tyrone Aiken looked at Dr. John Womble and asked: "Sensei, how did you overcome all the challenges of the School of Samurai?"

Born and raised in South Carolina, Aiken's childhood was solitary. After joining the United States Naval Oceanographic Office—while fulfilling his military service as a non-combatant at a rank of ensign—he traveled the world and eventually became a navigational scientist. In 1972, he attended Federal City College part-time as a student and quickly became interested in Dr. Womble's elective martial arts class.

When he went to the dōjō to learn more about days and times he would be able to attend Dr. Womble's class and see how he'd be able to fit it into his busy schedule, he discovered much more than what he initially intended to. He was met by Dr. Womble, whose commanding presence made Aiken swallow a painful gulp of air when he stood in front of the sensei.

"What can I do for you, Mr. Aiken?" Dr. Womble asked the younger student.

"I would like to take part in your martial arts classes, sir," Aiken replied, his voice conveying not the carefree lightness of youth that his age would have suggested, but the weight of the lived life of a man whose eyes were no longer naïve as those of his peers, because they had seen things that could never be forgotten nor erased from his soul's memory.

Dr. Womble stood silent for a few moments, studying Aiken's stance. Silence, Dr. Womble believed, could be the true carrier of meaning, as opposed to words often used to hide it.

"Where did you serve, Mr. Aiken?" Dr. Womble asked.

Aiken frowned, quietly questioning himself whether or not he had indeed told Dr. Womble about his time in the military. He was sure he had not. So, how did Dr. Womble know?

As if capable of reading his mind, Dr. Womble said, "I can tell by the way you carry yourself, Mr. Aiken. As a former military member myself, I recognize certain traits that only the military can teach a man."

"I traveled the world, sir," Aiken said. "Can't reveal much of my missions though because of how dangerous they were and who was involved."

"I understand and respect that, Mr. Aiken," Dr. Womble said. "Did you hear of the *USS Pueblo* capture four years ago during a spy mission?"

A shift in Aiken's eyes told Dr. Womble everything he needed to know about his would-be student.

"North Korea captured it," Dr. Womble added. "All eighty-two crewmembers were released, though one died during the capture."

"Yes, sir," Aiken said, his voice slightly betraying his composure. "I served on similar ships during the Cold War beneath the sea."

"I understand the dangers faced by soldiers and sailors serving in foreign countries and international waters, Mr. Aiken," Dr. Womble said. "And because of my own experiences, I hear also what you don't say about your time in the military. You traveled the world, huh? That to me sounds like you were in some of the most dangerous lairs that mercenaries, former patriots, spies, and criminals frequented."

Aiken lowered his gaze for a brief moment.

"You risked a lot, Mr. Aiken," Dr. Womble said. "It's a miracle you're still alive."

Aiken did not reply. Instead, he looked back up to Dr. Womble, who was looking at him in a way that made him feel as though he could read his mind and see his soul. It was in that moment that Aiken realized he would have to give this man his full commitment if he wanted to have a chance at learning from him. And he wanted to. More than anything.

"So why do you want to learn martial arts?" Dr. Womble asked him, still standing in front of him.

"I want to learn to defend myself, sir," Aiken said. "With the raging violence I have witnessed in Washington, DC, where being robbed at gunpoint or assaulted with a knife is no longer that uncommon, I want to make sure that I stay alive."

"Then go join someone else's class, Mr. Aiken," Dr. Womble said, turning back as if about to walk away from him.

"Why?" Aiken asked.

"I don't teach self-defense, Mr. Aiken," Dr. Womble said. "I teach much more than that. My students are here because they want to follow this way of life, not because they want to learn how to get out of a chokehold while walking back home. So, if that's all you want to learn, there are many other schools out there that will require much less commitment and dedication than my dōjō."

He began walking away when Aiken said, "No, sir, I don't want to join any other school."

Dr. Womble stopped but didn't turn to look at him.

"I want to learn from you, sir," Aiken said. "Anything and everything you can teach me."

"It won't be easy, Mr. Aiken," Dr. Womble said, slightly looking back at him. "You'll regret it, just like all the students who came before you and left my dōjō. You will have to work harder than you have ever worked in your entire life. Not just physically, but especially mentally and spiritually. I am possibly the most controversial and talked-about sensei there is in this country, the one who's most looked-down upon by my competitors who spend so much time researching me and my teaching methods, the one who gets more fingers pointed against them than anyone else I know." He turned around and walked back toward Aiken. "I will push your boundaries, and just when you thought you've reached your limits, I will push you even further, again and again. I will be demanding, unrelenting, and unforgiving with your training. There will be no shiny medals to bring home, no heavy trophies to raise on the podium, and no glory in newspapers and tournaments. Still want to join, Mr. Aiken?"

Aiken didn't reply right away. Instead, he looked at Dr. Womble's unwavering gaze for a few moments and then said, "How do I sign up?"

"Welcome, Bugeisha Aiken," Dr. Womble said.

Aiken wasn't certain, but he thought he saw the corners of Dr. Womble's mouth slightly curling upward as if attempting to smile.

From that day onward, Aiken became Dr. Womble's student. Through him, he gained control of not only of his body, but also his mind and spirit, and learned how these three entities worked together in balanced harmony.

One day, after months of training and learning about Dr. Womble's time in the School of Samurai in Japan, Aiken asked Dr. Womble, "Sensei, how did you succeed and graduate at the top of your class in the School of Samurai?"

Womble closed his eyes as if he was reminiscing. Then, after a few moments, he said, "Mr. Aiken, I followed instructions."

Aiken didn't fully understand what he meant by that, until months later, when he first recognized the danger of ignoring instructions.

It was 1973, and Aiken was a green belt. Dr. Womble told him he would have to face a more skilled, more confident, and taller opponent, who was also a student at Dr. Womble's dōjō. Aiken didn't hesitate. However, two minutes into the match, it was already over.

But on the ground, hurt, wasn't Aiken. No, the young student was standing in the dōjō, looking at his taller, more skilled, and more confident opponent whose knees were buckling as he stood there, disoriented, with his bare feet standing on the wooden floor.

"Did I kill him?" Aiken asked, but his voice was so thin nobody heard his question.

With a ridge hand toward his opponent's neck, Aiken had struck his jugular vein, which caused it to swell and turn into a lump the size of a ping pong ball. Basically, with one single move, Aiken had temporarily paralyzed his opponent.

"Sensei," Aiken said, this time louder for everyone to hear him. "I might have killed him." He stood there, looking at his opponent, who was still rigid on the floor. Aiken put both hands on his head in desperation, and as if talking to himself, he said, "I didn't think I was any good at martial arts yet. I didn't think I could be this dangerous."

Dr. Womble didn't reply to Aiken, nor did he give him any attention. For the moment, his focus was exclusively for his student who had suffered the injury. He tended to him and soon he came to, the injury finally subsiding to Aiken's great relief.

Dr. Womble stood up and looked at all the students present. Once he was certain he had their attention, he asked the student: "What were you doing?"

"I was trying a secret Kung-Fu move that could have struck a pressure point near his groin and paralyzed him," the student said, looking at Aiken.

Dr. Womble inhaled deeply. Then, with his thundering voice said, "How many times have I told all of you not to mix styles of martial arts?" Every student in the dōjō lowered their gaze, each one of them guilty, at one point or another, of not following their sensei's instructions. "This is not a sport," he said. "If you want to practice martial arts because you think it is just a sport, you are free to walk out of here and join other schools, just like many other students have done before you. Go ahead, train with them; at least you'll bring home medals." When nobody moved or hinted at wanting to leave his dōjō, Dr. Womble added, "Failure to follow instructions can have devastating consequences because it can cause life-altering injuries."

Silence blanketed the students as they all took in what it really meant to follow instructions.

Some time later, Aiken tested his boundaries once again by attending a full-contact tournament in Baltimore, Maryland, by himself and without permission from his sensei, who had no idea where his student had gone. Aiken had been attending Dr. Womble's school for some time now and wanted to test himself, to see just how much he had learned. For the first contest, he engaged a black belt and was stunned when his opponent bearhugged him and whispered, "Please don't hurt me."

In a following match, Aiken executed a well-controlled technique so quickly and precisely that the judges couldn't see it. When they questioned him about it and reminded him that only practical and pre-accepted movements were admissible, he didn't argue with them. Instead, he looked at the judges and said, "You cannot see what you don't believe is possible."

Though Aiken left the tournament with his head held up high, word quickly got back to his sensei, who didn't shy away from confronting him right away once Aiken went back to his dōjō.

"Bugeisha Aiken," Dr. Womble thundered. "Never attend a tournament alone."

"But sensei," Aiken said, "As you can see nothing bad happened, so why worry?"

"Because they don't like me," Dr. Womble said. "To retaliate against me and my school of thought, they will hurt my students on purpose. I always watch out for my students at these tournaments because they often allow opponents to execute illegal techniques, such as blows to the throat, groin, and eyes. And I don't want my students getting hurt or maiming or incapacitating opponents simply because of other people's unrestrained attacks and false confidence. Which is mostly based on demonstrations with imitation weapons and breaking fake boards. Either way, you may be accused of being vicious, or if you're the victim of illegal techniques, far too often judges are reluctant to intercede. That's why I need to be nearby. Understood?"

Dr. Womble's eyes conveying much more than his words did, for it was in them that the real weight and importance of his message was explained.

Aiken understood and respected his sensei's wishes, though he kept wondering what his life must have really been like when his sensei attended the School of Samurai. A few weeks later, Aiken finally had the perfect opportunity to ask him questions that he had never been able to ask him before. It was during a fishing trip to the banks of the Shenandoah River in West Virginia. Aiken waited until there were no distractions around, and eager to learn more of how his sensei developed his skills and perfected his training, a curious Aiken asked: "Sensei, what did you eat there?"

"We ate rice and fish eyes," Womble said, looking right at his student, the straight corners of his mouth conveying he was serious.

"Fish eyes?" Bugeisha Aiken echoed, his eyebrows raised and his lips slightly parted in surprise.

"Yes, and occasionally they would add plums," Womble explained, as if it were the most obvious thing in the world—an attitude that only left his student even more speechless. "Following instructions was one of the core principles of character building and we had to demonstrate our understanding and commitment every day. Those who failed were often met with deadly consequences. For example, at night, I once heard another student say, 'my father was a Kenjutsu master, and I know the techniques.' You see, he thought he knew better. The next day, he faced a master with a shin-ken (forged blade) and was instructed on what to do. However, thinking he knew better, he deviated and suffered fatal injuries."

Aiken stood there, quietly. Dr. Womble's answer reminded him of his own experience against the more skilled opponent who did not follow instructions and how his deviation, his ego, his I-know-better attitude almost cost him his life.

Then, Aiken asked, "What else can you tell me about your time at the School of Samurai? I know that dialogue was a pivotal part of your training, and you encourage us to ask questions, but what conversations did the masters focus on?"

John Womble looked in the distance, his gaze allowing his memory to travel back in time to when he was a young soldier in Kumamoto City. "Yes, mondo—or dialogue—was pivotal to our training as it stimulated our mind and spirit," he began. "I once heard my masters discuss matters of science, psychology, technology, toxicology, and Kabuki role-playing. But it wasn't in the way that most westerners might imagine these topics were discussed."

He paused, his student's attention undivided and unwavering. "They discussed swords versus guns and how visual and auditory intelligence and sensitivity are the best possible solutions to anticipating the actions of attackers. Rangers call this situational awareness—I say sensitivity to make it easier to explain. Aiken, remember to watch your six!"

The furrowed eyebrows of his listener told Womble that he needed to explain the difference a bit more in order for Bugeisha Aiken to fully comprehend it.

"They did not discuss Leonardo da Vinci's *Mona Lisa*; rather, they discussed how a karate master might kill a bull with their fist." Womble looked at his student, whose eyes were beginning to convey understanding. "For example, once they talked about killing a bull by rendering it instantly brain dead, so adrenaline and other chemicals would not affect the quality of the meat. My masters would challenge their students—including myself—to kill a bull or a wild boar as a demonstration of courage. If we hesitated, even for a second, we could be doomed because, when faced with a wild animal, you are placed in a situation of life or death."

John Womble went on to explain that he hunted wild boar using a boar spear[29], which is designed to impale the animal as it charges toward the hunter. He faced the boar with his foot on the end to anchor the spear into the ground while holding a rope to elevate the tip of the spear under the charging boar's chest. The idea is that momentum of the charging boar will drive the spear into its body up to a point where the cross piece stopped it from continuing toward the hunter.

---

[29] A boar spear is a short and heavy spear used for wild boar hunting.

"The meat of the bull that master Mas Oyama—a famous karate master who fought against bulls—killed was indigestible," Womble added. "But the other master's kill could be eaten. The comparative analysis between Mas Oyama and another master's technique was based on the taste of bull meat. The cause might be that the bull was not saturated with adrenaline—tough meat is associated with a stressed animal."

"Sensei," Aiken said, "Why did you not ask us to demonstrate our courage by facing a wild animal?"

"Because it is an illegal practice here," Dr. Womble explained, declaring that he was determined to find a similar way to challenge his students, and that is when he decided that his students would have to prove their courage by lying supine on two chairs, placing a cucumber on their stomach, and having him execute a vertical cut with a katana, cutting the cucumber in half. Only one student came forward. Aiken. He positioned himself the way Womble wanted him to, and the sword cut through the cucumber like a hot knife cuts through butter. Womble continued, "As Samurai, we were versed in many areas of sciences and arts. In addition, we were taught methods of meditation and Kata or movement that made the organs—especially the brain—function at optimal levels. Also, they understood macrobiotic strategies or dietary practices along with acupuncture and shiatsu principles. As a result of these teachings, we were able to limit the effects of the primitive brain, which can activate the parasympathetic nervous system, triggering adrenaline. As I mentioned in class, most of you are at the mercy of your organs. As the masters taught me, character is a product of environment, education, and legacy. Furthermore, learning Kenpo-Bujutsu is not suitable for all as it is a lifestyle as opposed to the sport version, which is a valuable alternative to those who wish to learn of some of the core values of martial arts but cannot commit to its challenging demands. The twelve masters taught us to observe and study animals—just like the old masters did. As you know, I kept a snow leopard in my barracks in Japan and trained army dogs for combat. The mysterious snow leopard is unique and rarely seen in groups or pairs like other leopards. Also, I brought my Doberman, named Major, back to the United States, as they cannot be transferred to another owner once trained and are usually put down. Currently, at my house, I have a black leopard, piranhas, a boa constrictor, and Yojimbo and Shiba—my dogs. From these animals, I've learned to expand my sensitivity beyond average humans. Ancient eastern and western history show that military leaders have always prized the warriors who were stoic in the face of death."

While explaining and demonstrating, he went to the edge of the riverbank with a machete to strike a snake feeding on our fish attached to a metal fish stringer anchored to the riverbank. "The masters assessed us on all fronts; they were unequivocal and determined to make sure their knowledge, skills, and abilities were only transferred to suitable vessels," he added. "You could say they had an encyclopedic knowledge of the eastern and western principles of molding a person's character into something greater or a Samurai—specifically, over twenty-five hundred years of eastern and western knowledge of martial arts and traditions. We studied sacred books that are the underlying seeds of civilization—the *Bible*, the *Koran*, the *Vedas*, the *Gita*, and the *Prince* and Sun Tzu and Clausewitz and more—and the philosophies that made up the School of Samurai, from the Lamas,[30] monks of Tibet, India, and China, to the Shaolin monks—the only Buddhist monks to practice martial arts." He walked back toward his student and said, "In addition, there were applied concepts that were derived from theories associated with eastern and western sciences.

---

[30]   Lama is a Tibetan word for a spiritual guide and master.

What we call the scientific method and what eastern science calls yin and yang—one based on logic and the other on instinct or observations of causes and effects. Using these esoteric practices, my teachers were capable of accessing parts of their brain that stimulates higher order thinking. Specifically, western cognitive scientists know little of the pineal gland."[31]

"The pineal gland, master Womble?" asked Aiken, looking up at him.

"The seat of the soul," he explained. "Unlike other parts of the brain, it is unpaired."

As the conversation went on, the master revealed that, while he was studying, most—if not all—of the physical training in the arts of the Samurai was illegal in most countries. "To this day," Womble added, "traditional martial arts teachers are still concerned about preserving their essence—from alpha to omega. Originally, attempts to transition from the art to the do were met with resistance."

"How so, master?" his student asked him.

"The use of body armor and bamboo swords and noncontact contest were perceived as fakery," Womble said. "However, practices such as killing animals and unprotected full- contact contest to test the effectiveness of techniques often left one or both contestants maimed or dead; this was an impractical situation. There needed to be a better way of preserving the culture and traditions of the Samurai. One of the greatest successes was the sport of judo."

"Sensei, I lack knowledge of the history of judo," Aiken admitted.

Womble nodded, acknowledging his student's statement. Then, he began traveling back in time through his speech, moving elegantly and effortlessly between two realms, two worlds, and two

---

[31] The pineal gland (the name is due to its pinecone shape) is a small endocrine gland in the brain that produces melatonin, a hormone that helps induce sleep.

ways of seeing and perceiving the same entity. He explained that in western culture, judo is often synonymous with showing physical strength over an opponent showcased in a series of rather dangerous movements that include choking, throwing, twisting, and bending the opponent's joints, among many other tricks—often leading to life-threatening situations. However, a look back at the philosophy, physical training, and meaning of this Japanese martial art—which has been popularized and espoused in diverse forms by over two hundred countries—proves that its original interpretation had less to do with physical superiority or dangerous practices. On the contrary, judo focused first and foremost on developing the student's mind and their mental strength and resiliency. Bodily strength and physical aptitude are simply results of the mental and spiritual training.

"When I returned from Japan," Womble said, "I did not just bring with me all the

physical training that I endured under the guidance of Dr. Chitose and the other masters at the

School of Samurai in Kumamoto City. I brought with me all the lessons of my twelve masters and their legacies: hundreds of years of knowledge from India, China, and other cultures—an inestimable encyclopedia of knowledge on resiliency, spiritual strength, and mental endurance."

He explained that Gōgen Yamaguchi (headmaster) and Gichin Funakoshi were among them, in addition to Dr. Chitose.

"No matter what course one takes, both traditional and martial sports require years of dedication under the guidance of a qualified teacher." Womble added.

Many of the pioneers in Japanese martial arts instruction were educators first and foremost, as it was important to be educated in order to make ethical decisions, especially in times of crisis.

"Judo is an excellent way of simulating crisis or responding to crisis of perception in order to act ethically in daily life. In other words, being deprived of one's balance is usually stressful—but judo encourages students to reconcile their relationship with gravity and balance by practicing falling," Womble said as his student listened intently. "Professor Jigorō Kanō was the first to create a way or ontology for transferring judo training into tangible benefits for the untrained. In May 1879, Kanō was part of a select group of martial artists that performed in a special event when President Grant visited Japan. He was lauded worldwide as the creator of judo."

As Womble stood before one of his masters, he was unnerved by his frankness—a kind of verbal judo designed to change his perspective or frame of mind and perhaps save his life.

"In America they hang your kind," a master had said.

Womble's perspective instantly changed. As a young Black Samurai, full of pride and confidence, his return to America was not going to be the same triumphant welcoming he had envisioned. But he was not the same person that had left for the military. He was now a Samurai.

★　★　★

Born into a wealthy family in 1860, Kanō was well educated but bullied in his childhood because of his small and fragile frame, as he was shorter and thinner than most of his peers. Kanō was introduced to the art of jujutsu as a way for him to gain physical strength and defend himself against bullies. He had some of the best professors in both eastern and western schools. His knowledge of western educational theory played a big role in developing judo, as he felt that education could change society. His curriculum was impressive—even by today's standards—as he studied English literature, world history, aesthetics, economics, western philosophy, Chinese and Japanese classics, Asian history, and much more. However, he soon learned that there was a lot more to overcoming an obstacle—be it a stronger opponent on or off the tatami—than just becoming educated and physically fit. One had to have, first and foremost, perseverance and mental strength or resilience. And those were attributes that training in jujutsu didn't necessarily teach him. The solution? He created a brand-new martial art, based on jujutsu but without the deadly techniques, and western educational theory, that would approach training in all its forms: mental, spiritual, and physical.[32]

And that was how judo was born. Kanō named his dōjō Kōdōkan, meaning "A place for the study of the way"— 講 (kō) translates into "to lecture," 道 (do) means "the way," and 館 (kan) means "a public building." To this day, the institute for the worldwide judo community, located in an eight-story building in Tokyo, is called Kōdōkan.

Jigorō Kanō once said that "Japan has learned various things from the nations of the world so far. Japan must, in turn, teach something to the world. In the future, if Japan teaches the judo I advocate, it will be able not only to contribute to world culture for the first time but also to assist in the international development of Japan, with those groups that have learned judo playing a central role."[33] Kanō's life-long dedication and commitment to the art of judo prompted him to

---

[32] "Ernest Fenollosa (1853–1908) was the professor who had the greatest lasting influence on Kano. Fenollosa had come from Salem, Massachusetts, to Japan in 1878 to teach philosophy and economics at the university. Under Fenollosa's four-year tutelage, Kano learned about modern western educational philosophy and later how important it is to appreciate the beauty and significance of Asian culture." John Stevens, *The Way of Judo* (Shambhala, 2013).

[33] Jigorō Kano, *Mind Over Muscle: Writings from the Founder of Judo* (Kodansha International, 2013): 8.

travel overseas thirteen times in the hopes of educating those willing to learn the true essence of his martial art. During his travels, Kanō witnessed firsthand how many people across the world reacted to difficult times by relying on dangerous and temporary forms of relief—such as alcohol, gambling, and drugs. When the effects of these unhealthy habits vanished, the individuals were not only still facing the same obstacle that had initially prompted them to seek refuge in harmful behaviors, but they were also worse off than they previously were because they now had to deal with the additional stress caused by their addiction, which led to mental anguish and physical malaise. And that's what Kanō knew he could help people with. Through his judo teachings and training, he would help them develop a resilient and determined spirit that, paired with mental tenacity, would eventually help them face and overcome any challenge that life threw on their path.

Kanō's main purpose in developing judo, however, was to advance education in his home country. He believed that "one must endeavor to preserve one's health, develop both a robust physique and a spirit of perseverance prior to the pursuit of one's objectives, for without these basic prerequisites, one can accomplish little of genuine substance." Intense motivation, undivided commitment, and perseverance were indeed the main focus of Kanō's teachings, as these three primary principles can be "inculcated in a trainee and further enhanced as a result of dedicated and disciplined judo training."[34] Kanō's judo had three main components:

- Randori: Free practice. Kanō mastered randori while training in jujutsu. Specifically, randori is the practice of "sparring sessions in which both participants practice attacking

---

[34] Watson, *Judo Memories*: xviii.

and defending, using freely applied throwing and/or pinning techniques."[35]

- Kogi: Lectures. A firm believer in the importance of education, Kanō felt it was equally vital to learn about judo and its principles through a series of lectures.

- Mondo: Dialogue. Perhaps one of the most distinguished traits of judo as taught by Kanō was his dialogue with his pupils, carried out through a series of questions and answers (dialectal reasoning).

Kanō was the creator of many techniques still used in judo training, such as the method he developed for breaking his opponent's posture. In describing how he attained mastery of the technique, he explained that, when training with Iikubo Tsunetoshi—a master teacher of jujutsu—after the death of his jujutsu sensei Iso Masamoto (1881), he would usually succumb to Iikubo, who was fifty years older than him—that is, until he started being the one to throw his opponent: "What I had done was quite unusual. But it was the result of my study of how to break the posture of the opponent. It was true that I had been studying the problem for quite some time, together with that of reading the opponent's motion. But it was here that I first tried to apply thoroughly the principle of breaking the opponent's posture before moving in for the throw. [. . .] The throw should be applied after one has broken the opponent's posture."[36] Aside from developing new techniques, Kanō also stressed the pivotal role that moral education played in judo training, for the ideal judo student-turned-instructor

---

[35] Robert W. Smith, et al. *Judo Kata: Practice, Competition, Purpose* (Via Media Publishing Company, 2016): 44.

[36] Jiichi Watanabe, *Secrets of Judo: A Text for Instructors and Students* (Tuttle Publishing, 2011): 35.

had to "understand how the principles of judo can be, by extension, utilized to help one in daily life and how they themselves can be of benefit to society at large."[37]

Roughly fifteen years after Kanō's death—which occurred in 1938 when he developed pneumonia while at sea—a young John Womble began his training at the School of Samurai under Dr. Chitose's guidance. At the same time, others were using Kanō's innovative way of reengineering the more dangerous combat systems into sports or do—such as karate-do, kendo, and kyu-do—however, judo was the springboard that made it possible to safely practice the concepts of the parent arts in the public domain. Dr. Chitose[38] and Gichin Funakoshi collaborated and created Chitō Ryu and Karate Do respectively.

The way or *do* can pave the way to the jutsu. However, the risk of fatal injuries is greater due to the combat techniques and practices—to include kicks, punches, and throws, along with the employment of live weapons. Traditional Japanese martial arts (Bujutsu), as it was taught in the past, is significantly riskier than any other sport, and it requires a qualified instructor and dedication. Even so, traditional Japanese martial arts, if taught in a responsible manner, allow people to excel in any area of life because of the emphasis on emotional and spiritual intelligence. Granted, some see traditional martial arts

---

[37]   Smith, *Judo Memories*, 69.

[38]   "One of Chitose Sensei's young school friends was Shoshin Nagamine, who would one day found the Matsubayashi Shorin-ryu style of karate, and become president of the Okinawan Karate Federation. One of their school teachers, later recognized as the greatest karate master of the twentieth century, was Gichin Funakoshi (1868-1957), the father of modern karate and founder of Shotokan. Another of Chitose Sensei's classmates was Funakoshi Sensei's son, Gikko (Yoshitaka) Funakoshi." The History of Chitō-ryū, Shuriway Karate & Kobudo Website, https://www.shuriway. co.uk/chitoryuhistory.html

like Kenpo Karate Jutsu,[39] Kenjutsu, and other arts of the Samurai as outdated considering the popularity of guns. Obviously, technology and society have changed; however, if the mental, physical, and spiritual forces can be channeled to empower bugeisha (exponents of Bujutsu) to accomplish greater advancement in arts and sciences, they can become of great value to their community. In a world of nuclear weapons, the way of peace is built upon the actions of everyone, every day, like in judo. For every action there is a reciprocal reaction.

John Womble mastered judo by adhering to Kanō's principles and brought the lessons he learned in Kumamoto City back to Washington, DC, at once inspiring disadvantaged Black youth to better themselves and fulfilling Kanō's wish that, one day, judo would become the essence through which Japan contributed to international development. A closer look at how Kanō's principles inspired Womble through the teachings of Chitose shines a light on how important Womble's years at the School of Samurai were to him. It also brings to the forefront what perhaps is the most important lesson that Womble learned—the importance of education—from both his primary sensei Chitose and other masters, a lesson that, judging by what Womble chose to dedicate his life to, clearly left a mark on the young US soldier while in Kumamoto City. As Brian Watson wrote, "Nothing under the sun is greater than education. By educating one person and sending him into the society of his generation, we make a contribution extending to a hundred generations to come."[40]

---

[39] "In January of the second year of Showa (1927) the head of the Kodokan, Kano Jigorō Sensei graced us with his presence in Okinawa. Mr. Miyagi Chojun as well as I spent two days performing demonstrations of Karate Jutsu Kata and explaining their meaning." Mabuni Kenwa, *Karate Kenpo: The Art of Self Defense* (Eric Michael Shahan, 2020): 55.

[40] Brian Watson, *Judo Memories of Jigorō Kano* (Trafford, 2008): xvii.

It was indeed the power of education that prompted Womble to reach out to young Black Americans living in some of Washington, DC's poorest and most challenging neighborhoods in the hopes of helping them become stronger individuals and contributors to society. Not strong in the physical sense—that would come at a later time—but mentally stronger, more resilient, and more driven. Compassionate and reliable individuals who would eventually become perceptive enough to understand a person's real intentions by looking at their body language as opposed to listening to their words. Womble learned to walk between the rain drops; in other words, there were times when he had to use his physical abilities as a Samurai while other times he could focus on the mental and spiritual training he had acquired and teach the gentle way to others who prioritized education and the health and safety of children and the elderly. A society can be judged by the way it treats the most vulnerable!

★   ★   ★

As the day came to an end and dusk began painting the sky with pastel colors, Womble looked at his student, who had absorbed so much wisdom from his master, and said, "Remember this, Aiken: education is the only prescription for a sick society."

And he turned to the sunset.

INTERLUDE

John Womble and the Samurai Dress Code

"Tell me something, Womble: why don't you ever wear a bowtie?" an older soldier asked John Womble as he adjusted his around his neck. "Don't you wanna look like a cool cat?"

The two men were getting ready to leave the base for a well-deserved evening off, but only one of them was obsessing over how well he looked.

"I don't need to wear a suit to be a cool cat," John Womble said.

"Alright," the fellow soldier said, glancing over at his younger comrade. "And you think that looking like you just gonna sell vacuum cleaners door to door's gonna help you look cool?" He was referring to what Womble was wearing: a pair of gray pants and a navy-blue sweater paired with combat boots. "Or you're gonna tell me that beauty is what's on the inside and it doesn't matter what you look like on the outside, blah blah blah?" he kept teasing in a singsong tone.

John Womble couldn't help but grin, entertained by this man's humor. Only once he was done tightening his bootstraps did he get up and walk closer to his interlocutor, who was still trying to adjust the bowtie.

"Perhaps you are asking the wrong questions, sir," Womble said. "Perhaps you focus too much on what I don't do—wear a bowtie— but refuse to see what I actually do."

The older man tilted his head and with all the naivety of someone who had never shared more than a quick meal with Womble, said, "Brother, what the heck have you been smoking?"

"To me, a Black man," Womble said, slowly pacing the small room he was momentarily sharing with his comrade, "a bowtie reminds me too much of the very object used by countless people before us to kill people like me: a noose."

The older man stared at Womble, his hands frozen on the bowtie that just wouldn't stay put.

"To me, a Black man," Womble added, still pacing, "displaying a smart look is not about looking like a cool cat, as you've so eloquently put it. It is about respecting and representing a code of conduct, one that has been followed by many Samurai before me for centuries."

"Did you just say Samurai?" the soldier asked, now even more puzzled than before, his facial expression conveying just how confused he was about this rather otherworldly exchange over what he assumed was a simple fashion statement.

"Indeed I did," Womble said, aware that his listener had not been initiated to Womble's dedication to the Samurai way of life (it had well surpassed the interest mark by then and landed confidently in the commitment mark). "Allow me to explain."

"Man, I gotta sit down for this one," the soldier said, making his way to an empty chair in the corner of the room, his bowtie still too loose to stay put.

Womble waited until his one-man audience was ready and then began: "A dress code represents a set of values, something that as a human being you uphold, believe in, and stand for. The comportment of a Samurai communicates to pedestrians the character of his lord, his sensei or teacher, family values, and ancestry. To the average American, independent thought and freedom of expression is paramount to freedom. To the Japanese, unity is most important, and gravitas is critical. Loss of face or shame is taken very seriously in Japanese culture. Failure to take social norms seriously or embarrassing oneself is like a sin against one's family, country, and sensei. We know how it feels to be portrayed as less but we fail to instill confidence and pride in our own young people. Therefore, it is no wonder that we remain in a cycle of poverty, ignorance, and despair. Personally, I believe in the Samurai code of conduct, which also includes a specific dress code. I do not wish to strive for equal opportunity; rather, I want to achieve higher standards than the American dream, I want to aim for so much more.

Judging by how quickly his eyes moved, the soldier certainly had many questions he wanted to ask Womble but refrained from doing so, sensing that his younger comrade was about to provide more details, and therefore, answers to his questions.

"For one," Womble said, marking one by raising his index finger. "The hair. It must be well groomed and pulled back so not to block eyesight. While the original hairstyle followed by Samurai in battle was hair pulled back and shaved on top so to minimize feeling heat under the helmets, the more modern version is pulling the hair back into a tight topknot called *chomage*. The Samurai now must be cleanshaven, although it didn't use to be this way. As a matter of fact, the longer the beard, mustache, and goatee, the more masculine the Samurai was and the more menacing and threatening he looked to his many adversaries. Just imagine that facial hair used to be so important in pre-imperial Japan, that some of the most famous Japanese warriors, such as Toyotomi Hideyoshi, used fake hair because he couldn't grow enough facial hair. However, it all changed when Japan transitioned from a feudal society into an imperial one and facial hair was no longer associated with power and strength but with aggressive behavior that became intolerable in such a peaceful country."

The soldier's expression resembled a perpetual question mark.

"Two," Womble said, raising another finger. "Every Samurai worth their weight will rise early every morning, bathe, and shave. No Samurai in good standing will ever walk around looking sloppy or unkempt."

"Sounds like the military," the soldier interrupted, although he did so in thin breath as if an inner thought had accidentally been voiced.

"Three," Womble said. "It matters to Samurai which colors they wear; Samurai cannot wear flashy colors that will catch people's attention. Rather, they must abide by a strict dress code that calls for subdued, somber tones such as gray and dark blue. Back in the 1600s, the Tokugawa Shogunate released a whole set of dress code rules that had been established for every class and social status, including the exact day in which people had to begin wearing spring, summer, fall, or winter clothes, regardless of whether the temperatures were cooperating or not."

The soldier raised his eyebrows, shaking his head ever so slightly.

"One could argue that these rules were enacted centuries ago, and as such, no longer bear any weight on today's Japan and its society," Womble said, finally stopping right in front of the confused soldier. "However, history has a way of seeping into generations and generations of people far removed from those rules, yet carrying the same traits within them, perhaps subconsciously. Still, those rules have now become so intrinsically unique to the very fabric of Japanese culture that one can no longer decipher where the past stops and the present begins. Even in this day and age, Japanese people care way more about what they wear and how they appear within society than most Americans do. It's more than a dress code like the one imposed upon us by the military. It's a way of life. It's a code of values."

Silence fell upon them. Well, actually, silence fell upon the un-initiated soldier who had just gone through his first *real* conversation with Womble, a man who often seemed unassuming and reserved, an introvert and mostly to himself. How wrong had he been in creating a narrative about a man with so much depth to his soul that one conversation just didn't seem like it was ever going to be enough.

He stood up, removed his bowtie, stuffed it in his pocket, and said, "My man, is there room for one more cat where you're heading?"

Womble nodded.

"Let's go then," he said, following his new sensei wherever he was going to go. "Just let me ask you one last question."

"Shoot," Womble said, walking outside the small room as the uncharacteristically chilly Okinawa evening sent a shiver down his spine.

"I get that you're following all the karate dress code and the clean-shaven look and stuff," the soldier said, glancing at their feet. "But I ain't buying that them Samurai wore combat boots too!"

Womble laughed a hearty laugh. "That's rule number four," he said. "Whatever you choose to wear, just make sure it's comfortable, brother!"

And the two walked into the Okinawan night with light spirit, choosing for once to focus on the laughter and not the war raging around them.

FIVE

John Womble could teach without speaking, inspire without moving, and win without fighting. Whenever he walked into a room, his steps were solid yet light, measured yet dignified, present yet reserved. His students could *sense* his presence even before they could see him physically there. His pragmatic nature would be unequivocally conveyed through his sitting position that highlighted his disciplined spirit and his mental awareness. Once each and every student mirrored his sitting position—which he would make sure of because sitting properly while meditating could lead disciplined students toward attaining enlightenment—he would begin to rhythmically utter, "Perfect vision, infinite wisdom, correct knowledge."

His mental calmness was even more impressive than his Samurai skills, which often caught his students by surprise—especially novice ones who assumed they were going to learn about martial arts from a screeching fighter and threatening sword wielder. But it wouldn't take long for them to realize that to be a true Samurai, physical skills are but 5 percent of their training. The remaining 95 percent can be found in training the mind and spirit—as without the proper mindset there's little chance of enduring the rigorous training of his program.

For it is in the mind that real fortitude can be discovered, and the most skilled Samurai is the one with an undisturbed mind.

While training in Japan, Womble was introduced to the philosophy of the Samurai mind, ancient lessons dating as far back as the thirteenth century when Zen meditation was first embraced by the Japanese warrior class. The Rinzai-style meditation that Samurai adopted and incorporated into their training was born in China—where it is referred to as Linji, named after Linji Yixuan, who founded the Linji school. This school remained basically obscure to Japan until the thirteenth century when the Linji school instituted koan contemplation. Koans are "cryptic and paradoxical questions asked by Zen teachers that defy rational answers. Teachers often present koans in formal talks, or students may be challenged to 'resolve' them in their meditation practice."[41, 42]

One of the main goals of Zen meditation was to become aware of life's most challenging questions, challenges, and demands. For example, a Samurai's main objectives included reducing fear of death

---

[41] Barbara O'Brien, "An Introduction to Koan Study in Zen Buddhism," Learn Religions (updated on February 11, 2019): https://www.learnreligions.com/introduction-to-koans-449928

[42] One of the most common koan: What is the sound of one hand clapping? While two hands clapping do make a sound, students are invited to meditate on the sound that one hand clapping makes. This question, like every koan, does not have a logical answer, and that is exactly the challenge. Students are invited not to reason about the answer, but to sit with the question until they become aware of the answer. Then, they have to present the answer to their teacher, which can be done without using any words and simply using body language or by making sounds. If the teacher is satisfied with the student's awareness, they will give the student another koan to sit with. If they are not satisfied, they will send the student back to sit with the koan again until they become aware of it.

on the battlefield by focusing on it much more often. Although this might come across as an oxymoron at first, the practice of inviting death into the mind with the purpose of reducing one's fear toward it was common amongst not only Zen Buddhists, but also among Greek and Roman stoics.[43] In fact, it was Epictetus, a Greek stoic philosopher born in 50 CE, who wrote that "death and pain are not frightening, it's the fear of pain and death we need to fear . . . So be confident about death and caution yourself against the fear of it."[44]

That is also how the Samurai used meditation to invite death into their thoughts in order to no longer fear it. Samurai Togo Shigekata said, "One finds life through conquering the fear of death within one's mind."[45] Meditation soon became a pivotal part of the Samurai's training because it was essential to achieving harmony within the mind. In order for the Samurai to attain success in battle, they had to learn how to stay calm by not allowing their emotions or thoughts to cloud their judgment. The state of complete mental clarity that every Samurai aspired to achieve is called Mushin no Shin, which literally

---

[43]   In ancient Rome, it was custom to celebrate a military general's victory in battle by parading him through the village on a four-horse-drawn chariot. The general, draped in the most regal clothes to include a purple robe otherwise only reserved for the emperors, was followed by a slave whose sole duty was to whisper two words in the general's ears: *Memento Mori*. Latin for, "Remember you must die," it was meant for the general to keep in mind that, even though he was victorious because he had defeated the enemy, he was still mortal, and death would eventually come for him as well.

[44]   "How To Not Fear Death," Dailystoic.com: https://dailystoic.com/how-to-not-fear-death/#:~:text=taught%20his%20students%2C-,%E2%80%9C-Death%20and%20pain%20are%20not%20frightening%2C%20it's%20the%20fear%20of,what%20we%20are%20doing%20now.

[45]   Rodney King, "Samurai Wisdom: Before the Battle," orderofmen.com (July 11, 2016) https://www.orderofman.com/samurai-wisdom-before-battle/

means "the mind without the mind." Accomplished through meditation, Mushin is "a state of mental clarity, awareness, and enhanced perception (sensory and intuitive) known as pure mind, produced by the absence of conscious thought, ideas, judgments, emotion (fear and anxiety), preconception, or self-consciousness. It is a state of total awareness and reaction not impeded by higher mental functions or emotions, a mind more open and reactive to subtle sensory input, intuition, and spontaneous action. It is a mind that is totally calm—a mind not influenced or caught up in events or others' emotions, thus a mind more able to freely perceive and respond."[46] By eliminating the distraction of thoughts and emotions, the Samurai became more present—and their awareness heightened—on the actual battlefield. It comes as no surprise; therefore, the arts and sciences of the Samurai are designed to extend the limits of attention span. In order for the Samurai to master the art of meditation, they spent significant time practicing it. First, they would concentrate on their breathing in order to vacate their mind of thoughts and their spirit of emotions that would interfere with their mental training; by using abdominal breathing, they were able to regulate the way they reacted to stress.[47] The focus on prioritizing and harnessing their state of mind was pivotal to their training, as a Samurai was expected to always be vigilant

---

[46] Christopher Callie, "Mushin: The State of Mind." Fightingarts.com, http://www.fightingarts.com/reading/article.php?id=62#:~:text=The%20Japanese%20term%20Mushin%20is%20a%20shortened%20version%20of%20the,fixed%20or%20occupied%20on%20any

[47] Perceiving or imagining frightening situations activated their brain's amygdala system—commonly known as the freeze, fight, or flight reaction that increases cortisol—and adrenaline for instant response. Samurai training encouraged reticence in the mist of battle. For example, a samurai armed with a katana can dispatch eight armed opponents in four seconds.

and could never be caught unaware or unarmed—something that has often been misrepresented in the West.

Once they achieved concentration, they would move on to a deeper level of meditation by reflecting on a koan given to them by their sensei. The koan may be a solution to the monk or Samurai's subconscious response to a perceived threat or childhood trauma. For most Samurai, this proved to be the most challenging part of their mental training because it was hard to sit with a given question. Some would call it a thought experiment, yet this was the only way for them to gain the mental fortitude and unwavering willpower that Samurai needed in battle. Once they sat with the koan long enough and achieved the level of consciousness necessary to offer their sensei an answer, they moved to a serene meditative state, during which their awareness of the moment was heightened, and they became fully aware of their surroundings.

But a Samurai was not just expected to know how to meditate and fight.[48] Given their primary role in Japanese life, they were expected to be well rounded in the arts as well. Calligraphy, for example, was one of the many art forms that Samurai had to study and master, and it was considered even more important than sculpting or painting—which were other art-forms that Samurai were highly encouraged to practice. Called shodo in Japanese—meaning "the way of writing"—calligraphy was often an indicator of one's social status because, the higher one's class, the more education one pursued. But calligraphy was so

---

[48] In times of peace, Samurai were role models of character. During feudal times, Samurai were, in some cases, judge, jury, and executioner. Subtle mannerisms could be perceived as insults, triggering instant retaliation. However, they were also held accountable to higher standards. Even today, Japanese people tend to mirror the patterns (kata) set in place hundreds of years ago by the samurai.

much more than class. The art of handwriting mirrored one's state of mind and revealed one's spirit. Therefore, if the mind and spirit were not at peace and properly balanced, devoid of unnecessary thoughts and emotions, calligraphy would reveal one's struggles and distorted mental state.[49] In the West, the pen is mightier than the sword. In the East, the pen and sword must be in accord, in keeping with the Samurai principle: bun bu ichi, meaning *mind and body in accord.*

The brush could therefore expose the subconscious mind, and for this reason, it was pivotal for the Samurai to achieve mental fortitude before dedicating themselves to the art of writing. "Each brush stroke in Japanese calligraphy must be perfectly executed since the artist never goes back to touch up any character. Each movement of the fude, or brush, is ideally performed with the full force of one's mind and body, as if one's very life depended upon the successful completion of each action. It is this spirit of decisiveness, of throwing 100 percent of oneself into the moment's action without hesitation, that perhaps most clearly connects budō and the art of Japanese calligraphy."[50] The spiritual strength that it took the Samurai to face the finality of the brushstrokes was not easy to gain and conquer. Just like in battle the Samurai had to be mentally and spiritually ready in order to be psychically prepared—for in battle there were no second chances, as death was the only other possible outcome. It was crucial,

---

[49] The same could be said for Shaolin monks. In June 2008, a Shaolin monk lectured on the history of the Shaolin monastery at the National Geography Museum in Washington, DC. He demonstrated how to transfer Ki or Chi or energy by asking several volunteers to lineup and individually punch him in the abdomen as hard as they could. After each blow, he instantly transferred the energy into beautiful calligraphy.

[50] H. E. Davey, "Budo and the Art of Japanese Calligraphy," Shudokan Martial Arts Association, https://www.smaa-hq.com/articles/article/3?articleid=3

therefore, for the Samurai to look at the brush before using it, because an unsteady brush revealed an unsteady mind. The Samurai firmly believed that the body was nothing more than a reflection of the mind and, as such, one could win over an opponent by understanding how to read their body language, because to them it represented the mind speaking. For example, if during battle the opponent's sword tip— which in Japanese is called *kissaki*—was not still, the Samurai knew that the opponent's mind was not still either. Their opponent's inability to keep their composure and void their mind of troubling thoughts and emotions was often the only indication a Samurai needed to know when and how to attack victoriously. The opponent might be an even better skilled swordsman than the Samurai. But if his mind was not ready for battle, his skills and physical abilities would be no match for the Samurai, whose mind and spirit were stable and in harmony.

In the same way, if the tip of the brush moved or shook, the Samurai's mind was not still nor ready to practice the art of writing. A wobbling brush would not only result in an unstable and flawed kanji, but it would unquestionably expose the nervous, troubled mind of its maker: "The Shodo student needs to strongly focus on the character to be painted for a split second, and then without hesitation, move the brush in a relaxed manner. In this way, the Shodo artist endeavors to succeed mentally before the brush even touches the paper, in much the same way that a skilled budoka will spiritually win before engaging the opponent. Japanese calligraphy dictates that the movement of a person's Ki slightly precedes the brush as it draws the character."[51, 52]

---

[51] H. E. Davey, "Budo and the Art of Japanese Calligraphy," Shudokan Martial Arts Association, https://www.smaa-hq.com/articles/article/3?articleid=3

[52] Ki, in Japanese means "spiritual force." Believed to derive by the energy of the cosmos, it is always present but will remain dormant if not cherished and taken care of.

Given the connection between Zen and the art of writing, it is no surprise that some of the most famous and successful calligraphers in Japanese history were Samurai. Their ability to achieve both relaxation and concentration was instrumental to the perfection of calligraphy. Yamaoka Tesshu, the founder of Japanese swordsmanship school Itto Shoden Muto-ryu, Ueshiba Morihei, the founder of aikido, and Miyamoto Musashi are only a few examples of sensei who mastered both budō and Shodo. These three sensei were experts at creating visible rhythm through writing dynamic yet balanced kanji:

> Each kanji has a set number of strokes that must be brushed in a precisely defined order. Within the form of each character, the brush should move smoothly from one stroke to the next. This creates a rhythm, which must not be broken if the character is to take on a dynamic appearance, and unless a constant flow of concentration is maintained, this rhythm will be broken. Many people have an unfortunate tendency to cut off their stream of attention at the completion of an action. In calligraphy, this often happens when finishing a single character or at the end of a line of words. It is vital to maintain an unbroken flow of Ki and concentration throughout the artistic act. In budō as well as Shodo, this is known as zanshin (literally "remaining mind"), and it indicates a kind of "mental follow-through" and unbroken condition of calm awareness. Shodo has been used in the past, as well as the present, as a way for budoka to develop zanshin without the presence of an actual opponent.[53]

---

[53]   H. E. Davey, "Budo and the Art of Japanese Calligraphy," Shudokan Martial Arts Association, https://www.smaa-hq.com/articles/article/3?articleid=3

Aside from shodo, Samurai also dedicated themselves to *chado*, meaning "the way of tea." The main purpose in chado was to appreciate and find beauty in simplicity. While western cultures often view a Japanese tea ceremony as a ritual made mainly of teacups, spoons, and slow movements, a closer look at this ancient tradition can certainly uncover its deeper meaning and explain why it is so closely related to budō and shodo. The true purpose of a tea ceremony begins even before the tea is poured into the cup. It starts with walking toward the sukiya, the tea house. As the Samurai walked along the roji—the pathways found in Japanese gardens—they would find themselves surrounded by greenery and irregularly placed stepping stones. The irregularity of the stepping stones forced the Samurai to be mindfully present in the moment because the pathway was not straightforward and, therefore, unpredictable—a metaphorical view of life and its uncertainty. The greenery enhanced the sense of beauty and invited the Samurai to void their mind of outside stressors. Once inside the sukiya, the Samurai were met with minimalistic simplicity that freed them of visual noise: bare walls, no decorations, and minimum furniture. The bare interior allowed them to focus on the very few objects that were temporarily displayed for the tea ceremony. As such, the Samurai were able to appreciate the few things that mattered the most in that moment.

Being mentally and spiritually present in the moment was also at the core of yet another important practice: *kado*, meaning the way of flowers. Commonly known as ikebana, the Japanese tradition of flower arrangements was pivotal to the Samurai's mental training. The Samurai, being pragmatic, sees the angles of the flower clippings, their positioning, as insights into the art of the sword (kenjutsu). This form of meditation required concentration and mindfulness, and the Samurai usually dedicated time to kado before battle. Just like chado, in kado, simplicity is the way to achieve beauty and encourage a calm mind and peaceful spirit. One masterfully placed flower can be even more beautiful than a bunch of flowers whose arrangement has not been carefully thought out and studied: "The minimalist nature of ikebana leads the practitioner to discover and appreciate every part of the plant (from roots, to leaves, to flowers, to branches) throughout its life cycle (from seeds, to buds, to blooms, to wilted and dried plants). While the use of seasonal, living materials leads the practitioner to contemplate the transience of beauty and life."[54] Originating in the seventh century when Buddhist monks began bringing flower arrangements to the altar, the practice of ikebana quickly reached the Samurai class.

Samurai were also expected to be sensitive enough to write poetry, specifically death poems Samurai would often write in the moments preceding their death—especially when death came as seppuku. The Samurai would meditate on his life and channel his emotions in writing, which was inevitably filled with memories, hopes, and regrets. Minamoto no Yorisama, a Samurai who lived during the twelfth century, wrote a death poem before committing seppuku. His poem read: "Like a fossil tree, from which we gather no flowers, sad has been my life, fated no fruit to produce."[55] A careful read reveals that Yorisama's biggest regret in life was that he never had any children.

---

[54] "What the samurai Knew about Arranging Flowers," Banabox.com (February 14, 2019) https://banabox.co/blogs/blog/meditation-through-ikebana-what-the-samurai-knew-about-arranging-flowers#:~:text=The%20samurai%20viewed%20each%20arrangement,big%20decisions%20on%20the%20battlefield.

[55] Steven Turnball, *The samurai: A Military Story* (Routledge, 1996): 45.

The practices of shodo, chado, and kado, and poetry were pivotal to the Samurai's mental training for they all required concentration and appreciation of the impermanence of life and the beauty found in simplicity. An open invitation to be mentally and spiritually present in the moment while voiding the mind of cloudy thoughts and emotions, they helped the Samurai achieve balance and harmony and, eventually, victory on the battlefield—which in turn brought honor to the lord the Samurai served. This led the Samurai to master the philosophy behind Zen meditation, which Womble learned, practiced, and absorbed during his years in Japan. He brought it back to the United States, where he guided his students in practicing meditation in order to achieve an undisturbed mind and a balanced and harmonious life.

What truly set Dr. Womble's school apart from the rest was his method of teaching Bujutsu, which was far different from other sports martial arts. Dr. Womble created a crucible that combined training in the dōjō and outside areas under extreme weather, as well as exposure to street attacks, and he occasionally recruited outsiders to attack or encroach on personal space to see how his students react. His methods were designed to filter out those who did not have the constitutions required for training in Bujutsu. Dr. Womble was always testing his students, even during their conversations, just as his own sensei did with him while he trained in Japan. It was for this very reason that his students, including Aiken, were subject to training any day of the year, whether during the day or night. The main reason behind such pressure was because Dr. Womble wanted his students to understand that martial arts was not a sport. It was a way of life, and as such, they needed to be prepared to call upon their training at a moment's notice.

However, Womble's students lived in an environment filled with distractions driven by businesses deeply engaged in conditioning the minds of consumers.[56] As a result, getting people to practice an alternative lifestyle that did not provide instant gratification was a herculean task. To keep them engaged while also imparting pivotal lessons, Womble often demonstrated his ability to fend off attacks on the weakest part of his body without sustaining injury or any changes in demeanor. His students quickly learned that landing a kick or punch was like attacking an oak tree—when students threw him, they were befuddled on how he could lighten his body and tumble as if he were as light as a feather. He moved in kata and with weapons as if in moving meditation. His eloquence in the language of movement created calligraphy in space and time. His organic patterns of energy told the history of the art in everything he did.

Womble also encouraged his students to engage in meditation, making sure, however, that they did not focus on the wrong thing—meaning, reaching perfection—but rather on what mattered the most: clearing one's mind of unnecessary noise.

"Mr. Aiken," Dr. Womble would say to Bugeisha Aiken. "You must learn to walk between the rain drops."

"What does that mean, sensei?" Bugeisha Aiken asked, unaware of the philosophical meaning.

"Eternal reflection will not result in perfection."

And with that, he voided his dōjō of sound and visual noise by practicing silence and encouraging his students to shutter their eyes

---

[56] Vance Packard exposed the types of advertising tactics used to encourage conspicuous consumption in 1957—a year after Womble started teaching—Vance identified eight compelling needs that advertisers promise products will fulfill: emotional security, reassurance of worth, ego gratification, creative outlets, love objects, sense of power, roots, and immortality.

halfway, not close them, and ready themselves to meditate. The meditative state was called metsuke. Samurai must be aware at all times even in meditation because the ninja or assassins were always vigilant. Closing the eyes completely leaves one vulnerable, so Samurai trained to be alert and perceive fine details while not being disturbed by sights and sounds of battle. Womble mastered the ability to live between the conscious and subconscious realities. His students followed his guidance. They were still and did not track or follow his movements or focus on him as if he were separate from the surroundings. Yet they knew he was there, for they felt his unwavering presence.

For his students, however, it would take years of experience outside the dōjō to fully understand the many ramifications of Dr. Womble's teachings and training. For Aiken, the opportunities to test just how much he learned from Dr. Womble presented themselves more often than he would have liked and in diverse ways he would have never been able to imagine.

"Which floor?" he politely asked two security agents who stepped into the same elevator as he had. After they answered, he pressed the button corresponding to the floor they needed to go to. However, he could sense the two agents were looking at him, even though he wasn't looking back at them.

"Hey," one of them said, "what would happen if I took those Gucci glasses, huh?"

Aiken knew he was talking to him because he was the one wearing the glasses. Aiken could have easily knocked this guy down, but that wasn't what he had learned in Dr. Womble's dōjō. A less astute and more arrogant person would have immediately fought back, either physically because he felt threatened by this security guard who had basically just insinuated that he wanted to rob him, or verbally, accusing him of what his real intentions were, just like school children on the playground. But Bugeisha Aiken had learned that first of all, he had to use his mind and acumen. So, before they reached the floor that the two security guards needed to get to, Aiken, in the calmest voice he could master, simply replied: "A blind man doesn't need glasses."

Bing.

The elevator doors opened, the two security guards walked out, and Aiken's lips curled up. He adjusted his Gucci glasses and waited for the elevator to reach his floor.

That incident, however, was far from being the only time he had to rely on his martial arts skills to handle a difficult situation. The incidents he was faced with did not stop at just verbal teasing, either. They became extremely dangerous, some of them putting Aiken's own life in danger. Some of these incidents involved Aiken's car. One day, while driving, rocks and cement were dropped from an overpass and crashed through his windshield. On another occasion, his car was intentionally forced close to the safety rail while he was driving on a bridge over the Potomac River, a clear attempt at killing him. It was thanks to his martial arts training that he was able to keep calm under such stressful circumstances.

When his attackers found out where he lived, one of them tried to force his way into Aiken's home. Aiken was quick to react and temporarily rendered his attacker unconscious. Then, he called the DC police and reported the break-in. When the police arrived at his house, the officers questioned him and when they were satisfied that they had gathered enough information on what transpired, one of the officers told Aiken, "You should have just killed him."

This was not the first time he received an insensitive response from DC police. Aiken had already published several articles and comments regarding corruption and malfeasance within local government. He testified before Congress, spoke on local television and radio, and published opinions about drug dealing, money laundering, environmental inequality, violations of the Hatch Act and sexual discrimination. In fact, the retaliation against him was severe enough to warrant a warning from Congress. On November 14, 1991, the US House of Representatives warned the EPA that retaliation against Mr. Aiken for testifying before Congress had consequences and any official of EPA that attempted to retaliate risked being fined up to $5,000 and/or imprisoned up to five years.[57]

So, when he was given unethical advice from local police, he suspected some form of passive aggression.

"That's not what I have trained for, officer," was what Aiken replied.

"But you've studied martial arts, right?" said the officer, whose raised eyebrows conveyed just how surprised he was by Aiken's answer.

"I have indeed, for decades." Aiken explained, "but being a martial artist is not what you see in the movies, at least not for me or anyone who has been lucky enough to being taught by Dr. John J. Womble. It's not about how high you can kick or how hard you can punch. It's about control. If you can't control your mind when

---

[57] Section 1505 of Title 18, United States Code, as amended by the Victim and Witness Protection Act of 1982, forbids anyone from corruptly, or by threats of force or by any threatening communication, influencing, obstructing, or impeding any pending proceeding before a department or agency of the United States, or Congress. In 1996 Congress enacted a clarifying amendment to 18 U.S.C. § 1515, which defines the term "corruptly" as used in section 1505 to mean "acting with an improper purpose, personally or by influencing another, including making a false or misleading statement, or withholding, concealing, altering, or destroying a document or other information." False Statements Accountability Act of 1996, Pub. L. No. 104-292, §3, 110 Stat. 3459, 3460.

challenges and obstacles present themselves, it doesn't matter how fit you are. You're always going to lose against your opponent. A lack of control over your mind can ruin your life."

The officers nodded to acknowledge they had understood what Aiken talked about. He thought about going one step further and explain to them that years of training in judo, karate, and other martial arts had taught him how to fall, how to perceive and anticipate attacks, how to gauge responses, and how to respond to fights with five or more people simultaneously. He had mastered restraint, compassion, self-defense, self-esteem, and had committed to continued practice that was necessary to be prepared for anything.

In one word, he had achieved *zanshin*, which is "the state when the mind is fully vigilant and aware of its surroundings; when the mind remains still without being attached to anything and is totally present during every moment and action in the here and now." While it is a concept that can be applied to everyday life and daily activities, such as eating, in bushido, "Zanshin means being aware of one's surroundings and enemies, while being prepared to react and being unaffected by pain. It is a state of mind that takes years of training to develop. Through the practice of meditation and martial arts, little by little, this kind of alertness can expand to every action of one's daily life, and in the end, one realizes that there are no ordinary moments."[58]

Aiken was often faced with situations in which he had to think quickly in order to solve problems with minimum complications, like when in the stairwell a coworker thought it funny to surprise him from below to test his reaction. He responded in an appropriate way, a measured use of force and persuasion in order to put an end to the

---

[58] "Zanshin," Zen Buddhism: https://www.zen-buddhism.net/zen-concepts/zanshin.html

situation before someone got hurt. Even when confronted with more aggressive attacks, Aiken, having learned from his sensei, responded with wit, unnerving potential aggressors in the most dangerous situations. Violence was never his first choice; only if attacked did he counter aggression in such a decisive way that it defied belief to the common pedestrian. Most of the time his presence and voice dispirited potential attackers.

"Make another mistake," Aiken would say to a potential attacker, just like Dr. Womble had taught him to.

INTERLUDE

Home Sweet Home?

"You must sit in the balcony," the usher told John Womble.

John Womble looked at the entrance of the movie theater he had decided to go to that evening. It was the 1950s and the golden age of Japanese cinema. *Ikiru* was the title of the movie, the story of a middle-aged man who, after being diagnosed with terminal cancer, sets out to find purpose to his life. A black-and-white movie in Japanese with English subtitles, the movie quickly sparked Womble's interest. He had recently been discharged from the US Army and sent back to North Carolina. Missing Japan and its way of life, Womble couldn't wait to watch the movie, which he knew was going to bring him solace and make him feel as though he were still in the country that had welcomed him as a son of the land.

"Why do I have to sit in the balcony?" Womble asked.

"Really?" the usher said. A white man in his early twenties, his breath reeked of tobacco and an air of superiority. "You need me to spell it out for you?"

John Womble didn't say anything. He simply stood there, in front of the usher, with his ticket in his hand, waiting for an explanation.

"Alright," the usher said, looking at Womble up and down. "Because people like you sit in the balcony."

"People like me?" John Womble asked. "What does that mean? Tall?"

"No. Coloreds like you sit in the balcony and use the coloreds' water fountain and bathroom," the usher said. "Remember? The place called the *crow's nest*. For Negroes."

There's the word. John Womble clenched his teeth. Tensions were high, and not just in North Carolina. Black soldiers had made their return home after tasting freedom and pride. As a result, they pushed back even more against the Jim Crow laws in the South.

"Sir," Womble said, staring at the usher. "With all due respect, I bought a ticket for this movie, and just like all the other people you let in and who are now sitting comfortably in the seats of their own choosing, I deserve to be granted the same kind of respect."

The usher opened his mouth to counterargue, but Womble raised his left hand and stopped him.

"You call me a Negro, but I don't see myself in that word," Womble said. "I am an American citizen who served many years in the Armed Forces, and even though I believe I earned the right to be treated as equal the moment I was born, if my birthrights are not good enough for you, then perhaps my decision to volunteer and defend this country and all its citizens—to include you, by the way—will be enough."

The usher didn't say anything at first. Instead, he helped many other people—all white Americans—get to their seats, making Womble wait at the entrance.

"Sir," Womble said, as he kept seeing person after person get ahead of him for no reason. "May I please go to my seat now?"

"Sure," the usher said, crossing his arms over his chest and looking at Womble with a smirk of bravado. "As long as that seat is in the balcony."

"I will not be going to sit there," Womble said.

"Then you can't go anywhere," the usher said.

"Sir," Womble said, inhaling deeply. "I will ask you one more time before I make my way to the seat that I paid for: may I please go and sit down now?"

"No," the usher said. "And don't you dare force your way through, or you won't be watching this movie at all or any other movie for that matter because I'll make sure they lock you up for a very long time. Ya hear me, Negro?"

That's it.

Womble stormed away from the usher and toward the booth where he had purchased his ticket. He stood in line again, waiting for his turn to talk to the man at the counter, and once it finally arrived, he explained his predicament once more. However, he didn't have any luck with this man either. Another white man, the ticket seller, uttered the N-word under his breath.

I have jumped out of airplanes and landed in enemy's territory for this country, he thought, as he felt his heartbeat increase with rancor. *I have risked my life for this country, every single day while I was part of the Army.*

He looked around and kept seeing people pass by him, as if he were invisible, and walk toward the usher, who welcomed them with a smile on his face and wished them a good time at the movie theater.

I served my country for all these people who now treat me as someone less than a human being, who can't even sit where he chooses to.

He had reached the limits of his patience and felt the flames of anger surface. The consequences might have been unimaginable had he given into his rage. But shortly afterward, behind his back, he heard familiar sounds of jeeps approaching the theater. Womble turned and quickly recognized the passengers: military police officers. One got out while the others stayed a respectable distance. A military police sergeant saw Womble and said, "Ranger, stand down."

Womble didn't reply, but he didn't need to. He knew what he had to do.

It was the silent respect between two soldiers that ended a heated encounter, one that could have gone horribly bad. Though eventually Womble cooled down and was relieved the situation had not escalated to the point of no return, he also realized something: long gone were the days when he was free to walk down the streets in Kumamoto City, attend a Kabuki show, and sit wherever he wanted to.

I was sent to another country to fight against a people who are deemed enemy to the United States of America, he thought as he stood there, motionless, in front of the military police officers. *Yet, the United States of America deem me as their enemy too.*

The injustice was too much for Womble to bear. While in Japan, he had become so enamored with the Japanese way of life and culture that he no longer felt like the Other. At the School of Samurai, he was one of the other aspiring students. Nobody told him where he could or could not sit. He belonged. But once he was back home, the one he had so selflessly served against his own mother's wishes, he was once again the Other. He no longer belonged.

It was in that moment that Womble came to terms with a devastating truth. His parting words to the man behind the ticket booth were: "Ikiru means *to live* in Japanese."

The cashier yawned, conveying just how bored he was of Womble's words, and perhaps his job and life.

But Womble added, "The man in the movie starts living the moment he receives the death sentence of terminal cancer. But at least, he's free to live his life the way he wants to in his own country. How will I ever live in this country if I'll never be free?"

Womble didn't receive an insight. He wasn't surprised though; he knew there was nothing constructive that man could possibly say—after all, why would the cashier go against a system that gives him power over others? Embarrassed, enraged, and mortified all at the same time, he tore up his ticket after staring deep into that man's eyes. The only thought that accompanied that experience screamed in his mind: *why was I sent away when our real enemy lives right next door?*

SIX

After decades spent in the nation's capital, Dr. John Womble decided to relocate to Ewing, New Jersey, with his life partner Deborah Frisby (DR Frisby) . Still very passionate about social justice and rectifying the wrong, Dr. Womble had no intention of slowing down, not even in his retirement years. In fact, he found new ways to apply the dictates of his oath as a Samurai and carry out his commitment to a life of service.

A firm believer in the power of the written word and the role it plays in revealing the truth and shaping the future, Dr. Womble became a reporter for the *Nubian News*, a local newspaper that focused on important issues within the Black American community—but that also had ramifications in the life of the nation as a whole. It was through his ability to contextualize facts and inform the public of pivotal matters that Dr. Womble advocated for the importance of Black history, the crucial role that community involvement played in the lives of those who live in it, and the Million Man March.

On October 16, 1995, Black men from all walks of life—college professors, doctors, waiters, students, athletes, grandfathers, little boys, and more—gathered at the National Mall in Washington, DC, to encourage support for one another and unite against social and economic injustices and struggles that afflicted Black America. Those present were asked to recite the following pledge: "I, [name], pledge that from this day forward I will strive to love my brother as I love myself…from this day forward, will strive to improve myself spiritually, morally, mentally, socially, politically and economically for the benefit of myself, my family and my people. I pledge that I will strive to build businesses, build houses, build hospitals, build factories and enter into international trade for the good of myself, my family and my people."[59]

Echoing the sentiment behind the scope of the Million Man March, Dr. Womble wrote: "Those that attended the March were, in every sense of the word, unique. Only those in attendance can understand what I mean; there was an aura that not only surrounded each person, but the entire mass of humanity that comprised the event. [. . .] I also think we must not look for any overnight changes. Remember, Rome wasn't built in a day. While we are preparing ourselves for changes, we might comfort ourselves with an answer to the longstanding question: Just what did you do in the Black people's struggle for atonement, brother/sister? We participated in the Rededication of Commitment and Purpose called: Million Man March. The most traumatic experience I had at this historic event was looking at and into the eyes of a lot of the participants, seeing and sensing peace, hope, and tranquility. To a degree, never before experienced in a crowd of this size. Although I cannot fully explain nor begin to understand how so many individuals from so many different places could exhibit such similarity of expressions, all in the same place. I believe only the gods can answer that one."[60]

---

[59]   Hamil R. Harris, "'Everybody wanted to be there.' Remembering the Million Man March at 25." (October 15, 2020) Washington Post. https://www.washingtonpost.com/local/million-man-march-anniversary/2020/10/15/91c151b6-0e77-11eb-8a35-237ef1eb2ef7_story.html

[60]   Dr. John Womble, "Million Man March." Personal archives. A few punctuation and capitalizations details have been altered for the purpose of this book.

An ardent believer in the importance of education—as well as in holding people in a position of power accountable for their own actions and the consequences those actions had on the community—he advocated for Ewing students by demanding accountability of the school superintendent for the poor SAT scores of Ewing students for over ten years.

"In the November issue of *Ewing People*, you said 'a number of new programs' will be in place at Ewing Township schools. Will these 'new programs' correct old problems?" Dr. Womble wrote in December 1995. "Were the causes of past problems determined before structuring these 'new programs'? If so, would you be so kind and share the facts brought out in your study with the residents of Ewing. Would you also share with us just how they will address these problems. Statistics show that for the past decade, the SAT scores for Ewing have failed to measure up to the national norm in the critical areas of verbal and math skills. I would be very interested in knowing what new program techniques will be used to correct same. It is my personal belief that the simple introduction of new programs without the specific objectives of correcting old problems is both naïve and irresponsible. It is illogical to attempt a resolution without first recognizing the problems."[61]

As Dr. Womble entered his late sixties and early seventies, he became more and more involved with the health care system in the Ewing/Trenton area. This was not by choice, but by necessity—and thanks to his education as a Samurai that allowed him to stay mentally clear and balanced even when recovering from multiple procedures to still advocate for himself and his fellow senior citizens for their right to be treated respectfully and to receive good medical care. Eventually,

---

[61]   Dr. John Womble. Personal Archives. A few punctuation and capitalization details have been altered for the purpose of this book.

his efforts to report their gross negligence paid off when the facilities at the hospital clinic improved greatly.

During this period in Dr. Womble's life, he received assistance from home health aides. He was alarmed when, through discussion with the aides and verifying certification requirements, he learned that home health aides were not required to receive vaccinations against seasonal influenza, tuberculosis, and other communicable diseases. He chose to verbalize his concerns for the potentially deadly consequences this lack of commitment and malfeasance of the Board of Nursing—the body responsible for certifying home health aides— could bring forth on patients like himself with weakened immune systems. He called and wrote letters to the Executive Director of the Board of Nursing, to the state senator for the district in which he resided, and to the then-governor of New Jersey. Dr. Womble explained why the lack of precaution and safeguarding on the in- home care team's part was detrimental to not only himself, but to the many other elderly patients that the certified home care aides served. Unfortunately, Dr. Womble did not receive the replies he had hoped for.

Dr. Womble spent his entire adult life advocating for the better- ment of people's life conditions and expectations. Not one to ever shy away from meaningful confrontation and conversation, Womble was a rare beacon of hope in his selfless devotion to serving others. Like a true Samurai, his life has been nothing short of a wonder, and his legacy, symbolized by his many students, allows his teachings to still show us the way of the Samurai.

INTERLUDE

The True Story of the Forty-Seven Ronin

"Loyalty, honor, and sacrifice are the three most important values in every Samurai," John Womble said to a room filled with young students who were eager to learn from the man they knew as the first African American Samurai. Rumors had been spreading across the nation's capital of the newly arrived man who spoke very little but whose mere presence was enough to intimidate even the most confident person.

"*I heard he trained for years in a secret School of Samurai in Japan where he learned things that no one else could possibly even imagine,*" one person whispered.

"*Oh yeah? Get this, while he was there, he ate all kinds of weird stuff,*" another said in thin voice. "*And I guess this stuff gave him like supernatural powers or something.*"

"*My brother said that he heard the Samurai's gonna teach all of his secrets to the chosen ones, and these people are gonna become Samurai as well!*" a young man said.

"*Man, I'm going to work so hard to make sure I'm one of them!*"

Indeed, the rumors about Womble had been spreading like

wildfire among the young and impressionable minds of tomorrow, which was why the room was packed. Sitting down with their legs crossed, they listened intently to every word he spoke as he slowly moved across the room looking directly at his audience.

"Any questions?" he asked.

A few of them looked at one another, surprised that he had already stopped talking to see if there were any questions.

"Dude, he said like ten words," one person whispered to the one sitting next to him. "Why would he think we already have questions?"

The other one shrugged.

But it didn't take long for one attendee to raise her hand. Everyone turned to look at her. *What could she possibly have to ask after such a short speech,* they wondered.

John Womble didn't say anything. Instead, he stopped walking and stood right in front of her. A nod was all it took to give her permission to speak up.

"Sensei Womble," she said, "Could you please give us an example of what the words *honor, loyalty,* and *sacrifice* mean to a Samurai?"

He didn't reply right away. Rather, he stood there, staring at her. To the surprise of other attendees who were also looking at her, she never looked away from his gaze. It was perhaps her determination and lack of intimidation that convinced Womble to reply.

"It was 1701," he said, as he began pacing the room once more. "Daimyō Asano Naganori of the Akō Domain was ordered to entertain people from the royal family who were coming to the Edo Castle. Asano, however, was not used to entertaining people of such high-ranking class—"

"What do you mean, he didn't know how to *entertain* them?" one attendee asked, eliciting laughter and innuendoes from other people in the room.

All it took was one side-eyed stare from Womble to quiet them all down immediately. Once the room was silent again, he said, "Etiquette, young man. Court manners and rituals one must obey and follow in an impeccable way, especially in Japan. It would do you good to learn some." Now Womble was the one making others giggle. "As I was saying, daimyō Asano didn't know how to properly host emissaries from the royal family, so he asked the Shogun for suggestions on how to best go about it. The Shogun was quick to recommend Asano go seek the help of Kira Yoshinaka, the master of ceremonies of the Shogunate who had previously instructed other daimyō on how to follow proper court etiquette. Asano did as he was told, but he soon learned that dealing with Kira was not going to be easy."

"Wait, why not?" a young man asked.

"Patience is a virtue," Womble replied.

"What do you mea—" he couldn't finish his question because he was elbowed in the arm by the man sitting next to him.

"It means that if you let him tell the story, you'll learn why," the man said.

The impatient man mouthed *sorry*, and Womble was able to continue his story.

"Kira was worse than a bully. He mocked Asano, degraded him, and harassed him. Asano did his best to avoid confrontation and tried to not pay attention to his incessant bullying and his bribing requests. But every man has his limits, and one day Asano reached his. After Kira's most savage verbal attack yet, Asano confronted Kira in the audience hall of the Edo Castle, where he unsheathed his dagger and slashed Kira's face, causing a large cut."

"Holy sh—" Another elbow in the arm stopped the impatient man once more. *Sorry* was mouthed again, and Womble continued.

"Though losing patience with a bully is a normal and understandable reaction in any human being, it is crucial to remember that Asano was no common human being," Womble said. "He was a Samurai, and being a Samurai meant that one had to embody virtues that went well beyond human nature. Being a Samurai also meant that he belonged to a higher, more important bloodline, and with the Samurai, so did his entire family. Losing his patience and attacking another daimyō, not only meant that Asano had not behaved like a Samurai, but it also bestowed upon his family something that no Japanese man nor woman could possibly live with: dishonor."

Silence.

No questions, no interruptions.

They're finally enough into the story that all they want to do is listen, he thought.

"Dishonor, when it came to being a Samurai, was worse than death," he said. "Asano went to the Shogun and asked what he had to do to fix the situation, and he was told that only committing seppuku would bring honor to his family again. So, Asano grabbed his dagger and slashed his stomach open, from left to right, killing himself." Womble could see that the idea of committing suicide in order to regain honor was foreign to many of his students, especially because it was in direct contrast to more Christian teachings that see suicide as a sin. Still, he continued with the story. "By committing seppuku, Asano was successful in bestowing honor on his bloodline once again, but he also left hundreds of Samurai without a master, thus making them all ronin. Let me tell you something: if you're a Samurai, becoming a ronin is the worst-case scenario because you're basically unemployed. As a Samurai, your whole purpose is to serve your master and if you no longer have a master, it means you failed in your mission to serve him. You're damaged goods. You can't just simply go look for another master because you should have protected the one you had. Who wants to hire somebody who's clearly failed in their mission? Still, forty-seven of the hundreds of Asano's ronin were not worried about employment. They wanted only one thing: to avenge their master's honor and kill Kira."

Gasps echoed across the room.

"But these forty-seven ronin knew that Kira expected them to carry out revenge against him, so they came up with a carefully planned strategy," Womble said, pleased to see he still had the attention of his students. "Phase one consisted of dispersing: some of them became merchants, others spent time in bars drinking way too much, and others . . . well . . . let just say they sought the company of multiple women."

Cheeky laughter could be heard across the room.

"Kira, who had hired extra guards and sent spies to keep an eye on the ronin, became more and more confident, as time went by, that these disgraced former Samurai did not want to avenge their master after all. Especially because he heard that the ronin leader, Oishi, had been found passed out drunk in an alley—where a Samurai kicked him in the face and spat on him, disgusted to see that a fellow Samurai could behave so poorly. So, Kira thought, *if their leader is behaving that way, I certainly have no need to worry about the ronin whatsoever!* But that's where he went wrong."

The students stared at him, waiting for more.

"What Kira couldn't have possibly imagined was that Oishi knew exactly what he was doing, and this was all part of his well-crafted plan. You see, Oishi wanted Kira to think that the ronin had forgotten all about their master, so he made sure that he and his fellow ronin acted accordingly. Oishi wanted the spies to go back to Kira and tell him that the ronin were just a bunch of men with loose morals and a passion for alcohol. And then, once Oishi was certain that Kira was no longer expecting revenge by the hands of the ronin, he and the other forty-six men, to include his own sixteen-year-old son, got ready to attack! But first, Oishi divorced his wife and sent her and their other children away, so that the dishonor that would certainly follow the killing of Kira would not fall upon them."

Womble could see a few heads shaking in disbelief, lips parted in shock, and eyes wide open with interest.

"Do you want to know what happened next?" he asked. He didn't have to wait long for a reply because a resounding *Yes!* jumped from wall to wall. "A year and a half after Asano's death, his forty-seven ronin stormed Kira's residence, savagely attacking his guards and making their way through. Each ronin knew that they would more than likely lose their life, so they fought as if they had nothing to lose—because they didn't. When they finally reached the inside of Kira's house, they only found women and children. No Kira. But Oishi went to his sleeping quarters, knelt beside the futon that we call a bed, and touched it: it was still warm. This meant that Kira was close. Very close, in fact. The ronin kept fighting against the guards and eventually Oishi found a secret path that led to a small building. Followed by his ronin, Oishi entered the building and eventually found a man hiding, crouched down. 'What's your name?' the ronin asked him, but he refused to say his name. But Oishi didn't need to hear what his name was; he knew he was staring at Kira, the man with the scar on his face. Oishi looked straight at Kira and said, 'I give you the chance to keep your honor by committing seppuku with Asano's dagger, the same he used to kill himself'. But Kira refused."

Womble paused.

The tension in the room was palpable because Womble had told the story with so much drama.

"What do you think happened next?" he asked.

"He killed the living sh—" *Elbow.* "Out of him."

Womble couldn't help but laugh. "Yes, he did. He beheaded Kira with the dagger used by Asano to commit seppuku. Then, he took the enemy's head to Asano's grave and told his master that he had carried out the revenge that would bestow upon Asano honor once again."

"So cool!" one of them said.

"But wait," the young woman who had asked the first question said. "What happened to the ronin? Didn't they lose honor because they carried out a murder?"

"When I come in contact with young inquisitive minds, I have hope for the future," Womble said. "Another good question. And yes, they brought dishonor upon themselves because they killed someone. But it wasn't an easy decision for the Shogun to make, because he understood why they did it. Snow was on the ground when the murder was carried out. By the time the Shogun had made his decision, cherry blossoms were delighting onlookers with the promise of spring. There was only one way for the ronin to gain honor again."

"Seppuku," said the impatient young man. This time, there was no elbow in his arm.

"Indeed." Womble said, "The forty-six ronin sat together and committed seppuku. The forty-seventh was spared so he could tell their story. They were all buried close to each other. Soon after, the news of their death spread across the nation, and it reached the ears of a Samurai who suddenly realized what he had done. That Samurai, who had kicked Oishi in the face and spat on him, went to his grave and prayed for forgiveness. Then, he committed seppuku and was buried with the other forty-six ronin. Their resting place is in a temple that can be visited today. So, if you ever go to Japan, stop by and take the time to say a prayer for the ronin, who embody the three main values of a Samurai: honor, loyalty, and sacrifice."

Speechless was an understatement for how the students felt. Silence fell upon them as they digested the story and what it meant. With a new understanding and better comprehension of the nature of a real Samurai, they looked at John Womble with renewed appreciation. Now they knew that he was truly the first African American Samurai.

SEVEN

"You must become better than me, don't make my same mistakes, and take the system to a new level." This was John Womble's message to his students, one he repeated often because he knew that as a master, his true limits were measured by how well his students would perform in the real world, not sporting events. To Womble, it was never about a black belt or how many trophies his students would display on a shelf. Womble knew that the real test for his students was life itself and how well they would be able to apply the lessons they learned and the wisdom they gained through him to their communities to create a better and safer place for the children and the elderly.

Unfortunately, many of his students fell prey to the stressors of real life when the draft, parenthood, jobs, racism, discrimination, assaults, rapes, and blackmail came knocking on their doors. Some simply had no time to train because of the many responsibilities they faced at home and work, some turned to alcohol and drugs, some died of AIDS, some faced violence in the workplace and succumbed to it. Others understood that there was only one way for them to fight against racism and to carry on his legacy and fulfill his dream of making a significant change: being able and willing to take on people, institutions, and governments to right the wrongs and stop the injustices.

It was after this pivotal realization that John Womble's students pulled up their sleeves and began applying all of Womble's teachings to better life conditions within their own communities. Their accomplishments are many and varied: they resolved some of the toughest problems, such as ensuring pesticides are safe, developing programs and laws to fight discrimination and racism in the workplace, providing recommendations to improve cybersecurity/national security and social services, and working in disaster areas as a FEMA reservist. In addition, they pioneered a task force to fight opioid addiction, worked with state officials to improve public school safety, and served in Europe as a visiting professor teaching environmental science, labor relations, and professional project management. They continue to teach martial arts, protect their communities by supporting law enforcement reform, and developing initiatives to reduce crime and child abuse. Chief among them are Tyrone Aiken, Steve Potts, John DeLoatch, Keith Pardieck, and Deborah Frisby.

In 1980, Aiken was hired by EPA as a chemist in the Office of Pesticides, a noble mission aimed at protecting the health and safety of people all over the world depending on pesticides to fight malaria, kill and control threats to food supplies, and provide protection against viruses.

"Aiken," Dr. Womble told his student when he learned of his new job. "Become the administrator of EPA!"

His request seemed impossible to Aiken, who thought it was absurd for him to go from a recently hired chemist to administrator. However, knowing Dr. Womble, Aiken understood that his invitation was not specifically to become the actual administrator, but to dig deep and find out how else he could help. So, Aiken meditated and realized there was more than one way to be a leader. He assessed the organization and saw gifted employees being undermined by unqualified managers, lack of access to technology, sexual and racial harassment, and bottlenecks in work processes, while many supervisors were encouraged to maintain the status quo. Fortunately, Aiken's supervisor was exceptional and felt no need to micromanage or keep employees occupied with busywork. He encouraged innovation and cultivated leadership.

Aiken chose to win the hearts and minds of his coworkers and managers by leveling the playing field, thereby creating an army of supporters behind the scenes intent on creating a better workplace. It was through their support and Womble's guidance that he became a legend at EPA. His accomplishments were due to support from federal employees and others from all parts of the government both state and federal and numerous organizations, including the US Congress, OPM, NASA, Department of Justice, Department of State, the Department of Education, and Harvard Kennedy School innovations program.

It is therefore no surprise that Aiken became the first African American president of the United States Environmental Protection Agency (EPA)'s professional union (NFFE–2050), the first African American president of George Washington University's graduate school Project Management Institute (PMI) chapter, and the recipient of the EPA silver medal for service on the EPA administrator's workgroup, where he played a key role in developing one of the most comprehensive policies on diversity. Aiken also leveraged knowledge he gained from his time in the US Navy to transform EPA in 2004, pioneered the use of IBM PCs, and automated the processes within the Office of Pesticides. He also spearheaded a regulatory initiative to determine the accuracy of pesticides and drugs around the world.

However, despite the support of his supervisor and several in senior management, he was denied recognition and the cash award as specified in the federal suggestion program. It took many years of legal action for Aiken to finally achieve recognition for pioneering IBM desktop computers in the Office of Pesticides and the pivotal role he played in saving the government millions of dollars per year because of process improvement—which improved performance of the program in achieving an efficient and effective process of certification of pesticide products designed to protect the national food supply, as well as human health and welfare.

After being summoned by a diversity workgroup within EPA to help end the unproductive discussions about defining diversity, Aiken applied root cause analysis and tactics he learned from Womble's lessons on Sun Tzu and total quality management (TQM) to address systemic barriers to minority and employees with disabilities. Eventually, he was successful in creating a way for them to gain access to high-profile projects. He modeled his system, Project Announcement Visibility Effort (PAVE), on the ideas from a professor of project management at George Washington University (GWU) and Dr. W. Edwards Deming, the founder of TQM. Unfortunately, Deming's many accomplishments went unappreciated in the United States, but he was embraced in Japan as a national treasure where he taught the postwar country of the Rising Sun how to rise from the fire like the phoenix to excel economically beyond belief. The idea is now a federal government wide system (Open Opportunities).[62] Currently more than two million federal employees can access the system.

But before becoming a leader in fighting for the rights of employees and expert of pesticide chemistry and computer science, Aiken was Womble's junior student, and it was an interaction with his master that proved to be the catalyst to Aiken's lifelong commitment to the

---

[62] https://openopps.usajobs.gov/

betterment of his community's life conditions and expectancy. No matter how many honors he achieved outside the dōjō, Aiken never forgot his loyalty to his sensei and remained in contact with him daily to stay focused. Womble didn't just remind his students that his knowledge was unlimited, he demonstrated it time and time again.

One day, Aiken excitedly mentioned to his master that he was taking classes from nationally recognized professors in toxicology. Womble, intrigued, inquired if he could attend the class as a guest and, after the professor granted him permission, Womble was able to take part in the class. The professor began talking about the lethal dose of alcohol and Womble started smiling.

"I see from the smile on Dr. Womble's face that he knows where I am going with this lecture," the professor said to the class.

He acknowledged what Womble already knew: the lethal dose of alcohol is the same dose required to become drunk, a horrifying discovery to many students who had no idea that being drunk meant being close to death. When the classes ended, Womble and Aiken walked down the hall, which the janitor was cleaning with ammonia. Suddenly, Womble stopped walking, catching Aiken's attention.

Aiken turned back to look at his master, who said: "Aiken, I can't believe you just finished attending a class on toxicology, yet you're walking callously into the fumes of ammonia."

Aiken's mouth went dry.

"Isn't this a toxic substance whose fumes can instantly affect your health?" Womble asked him.

This conversation prompted Aiken to become more conscious of what was around him and the perils that he, and other human beings, faced every single day. It was not just about sniffing ammonia. It was about sniffing all the other toxic metaphorical substances that society threw at him: discrimination, racism, sexism, fraud, and waste. But not everyone appreciated his stance. On the contrary, many fought to silence him as they were afraid of the unprecedented progress that he had the potential of bringing to society. For years, Aiken faced countless attempts to intimidate, retaliate, and undermine his work and his own life. Many around him wondered how anyone could withstand the continual emotional and sometimes physical intimidation and bullying with such composure. Still, Aiken persevered and became a whistleblower on fraud and waste in EPA, exposing and combatting discrimination and corruption in labor unions.

Finally, Aiken received severely belated and highly deserved recognition from his nation when he was awarded the silver medal for diversity, bronze medal, awards, and certificates for his innovative work. His name appeared in the newspapers, on local radio stations, and on CBS' *Nightline* led by Connie Chung. His most impressive accomplishment, PAVE, proved to be useful in focusing volunteers within the federal government to address crises and cross-agency projects. His efforts at PAVE provided a platform for federal employees to volunteer during the Hurricane Katrina and Hurricane Rita crises, where public health officers especially appreciated the opportunity to volunteer to go to the sites of disasters and assist without having to resign from current positions. Now, the system is being proposed for overall implementation as the future design of the federal workplace of the twenty-first century. And now OPM is implementing, in part, Aiken's initiative throughout the entire federal workforce as the open opportunities system.

Aiken has been a great source of inspiration to peers and younger generations to uphold, champion, and protect the same Samurai values and standards that Womble taught him. It was Womble who introduced a young Steve Potts to Aiken. During a TQM training session at EPA, Steve Potts asked Womble if it was still possible for someone to become a Samurai in today's world. Womble smiled and introduced Potts to Tyrone Aiken, whom he saw as the living embodiment of Womble's Samurai teaching.

Though Potts didn't know what to expect when Womble encouraged him to study under Aiken, after a few classes, he understood that Aiken had physical and mental capabilities that most found impossible to imagine. He suffered no fools and was not patient with students who lacked willpower. Nonetheless, Potts was not easily distracted or discouraged and succeeded in becoming a student-master after over twenty years of training, during which he endured hours of training in cold, hot, and challenging environments and acted with dignity and composure as he remained focused on his commitment to training, like the example set before him and his memories of Womble. He accomplished an advanced degree in science and was so impressive that Johns Hopkins professors recommended pursuit of doctoral studies. He gained respect for his knowledge of TQM and water pollution policies, and he assisted Aiken in projects that changed the federal and state governments.

He played a pivotal role in pioneering the federal government's design of the No Call list and appeared in local newspapers discussing the state of Maryland's hearing on preventing unwanted telemarketing calls and associated fraud targeting the elderly, in particular. He was pivotal in getting Congress and the Office of Personnel Management to endorse and implement PAVE and once the endorsements occurred, the initiative was posted on the White House website as an exemplary innovation for state and federal organizations to use.

Potts supported the gang task force in Maryland, which focused on the gang activities (such as MS-13 and others) that threatened the safety and longevity of the communities in the metropolitan area. He served as a court-appointed advocate for children in foster care where his knowledge of strategy came into full force tackling the failings in the system—these children were at the bottom of the scale in terms of support and were the most in need of protection, as they had no safety net and were often traumatized. He advocated in support of changing the policy to prepare children in the system who aged out at eighteen and were summarily ejected into society with no training in life skills like personal finance, student loans, communication skills, and how to gain additional health care and counseling if needed. He confronted judges, politicians, and organizations without hesitation about the abuses and mistakes leading to further victimization of the most vulnerable in society, a fight he based on Womble's oft-repeated maxim that "the purpose of martial arts is to help people."

Over the years, Potts has taught college students in Europe as a visiting professor and as part of an elite program partnered by the EPA and the Danish government. He taught traumatized students in Kosovo how to use TQM, project management, and environmental science to improve their communities and, not surprisingly, he quickly received a request to return. Currently, he serves as a reservist for FEMA in areas where environmental disasters have destroyed property and traumatized citizens. At the time of this writing, he is working with his congressional representative to ease the process for securing visas to go provide humanitarian help in Poland or Ukraine to victims of the war. But perhaps his biggest and most significant accomplishment is that, for over twenty years, Potts assisted his master in teaching martial arts as a path toward better health and a way to learn self-defense as well as how to protect children and the elderly.

Youngest among the students trained by John Womble himself, and crossing paths with Steve Potts and Tyrone Aiken, was John DeLoatch Jr., who far exceeded anyone in performing Kata and fighting skills in the Kenpo-Karate system. At seven years old, too young to attend, DeLoatch used to peer through the window of the East Capitol Recreation Center watching Womble train and practice and when he matured and developed more interest, he explored other martial arts classes taught by other instructors but found them lacking, noticing that every time he mentioned Womble to others, he would see the respect the community had for his martial skills and character. So, he gained enough courage to ask Womble if he could join his class and Womble happily accepted him at the age of nineteen.

After years of study and training, he reached the rank of fighting master and his performances of kata before audiences drew applause and recognition. He could have had a successful career teaching martial arts as a business, but his master taught him that the martial arts are not a sellable skill. Rather, it's a lifestyle not a business. Because of Womble's influence as a teacher and community leader, DeLoatch became a public-school teacher and for over thirty years, he has taught health and physical education, which he elevated by showing students the importance of character building. He currently researches the effects of martial arts and exercises to rehabilitate and reverse the conditions that lead to common modern health complications like high blood pressure, diabetes, and obesity. He also trains and practices the Kenpo Bujutsu system in addition to several sophisticated weapons. Such as, the sword, sai, tonfa, bo, and jo. He has proudly and successfully carried on John Womble's legacy for more than forty-five years.

One of the most recent students of the Kenpo system is Keith Pardieck, who studied under the tutelage of both Tyrone Aiken and John DeLoatch. Pardieck has several years of study in martial sports and in the last fifteen years he has achieved success up to a fourth-degree black belt in Kenpo Karate. His accomplishments in the community are exceptional, as he has led the establishment of a community-based oyster restoration program to increase environmental awareness and community action that now serves as a foundational part of the Calvert County Public School's environmental education program, and it has served over six thousand students to date. Pardieck is a part-time town councilman and leads their Opioid Task Force, which addresses the opioid epidemic rampant across the United States of America. His efforts to raise opioid abuse awareness, reduce stigma, and connect those in need with available resources in his community produced results, reducing the number of overdoses and deaths as compared to neighboring areas, and drew statewide attention. He also established an annual community health and wellness fair to emphasize the importance of proper nutrition, exercise, and health care for everyone, including those suffering from opioid use disorder.

He is a federal employee, a supervisory biologist, and community worker. He is also committed to teaching Kenpo Karate-Do to children, and he is an assistant instructor for the adult class.

Among the most devoted to John Womble's legacy is Deborah Frisby, the soul of the Kenpo Bujutsu. Ryu, the keeper of its historical records, and Womble's lifelong partner who supported him throughout his life and played a pivotal role in the success of his efforts and his legacy. She selflessly served her community, persevered through all odds, and always strove to exhibit the highest of standards, while dedicating her life to teaching preschool children, helping them keep their zeal for learning and integrating Black history into the curriculum. She became a skilled trainer/facilitator working at Associates for Renewal in Education (ARE) in Washington, DC, and developed criteria for choosing books portraying positive messages and images of Black children, which were published in Washington, DC.

Frisby helped organize a book fair that allowed preschool and daycare teachers and parents to buy quality children's books about African Americans and Latinos at a discount. She also organized workshops held at the book fair featuring renowned people such as Dr. Bernice Johnson Reagon, a musician, producer, and activist against racism, and well-known children's author Eloise Greenfield. But her commitment to her community did not stop there. She became a parent involvement specialist in the DC tri-state area for Head Start programs, where she carried out training sessions aimed at empowering parents to be positively involved in the education of their preschool children. She was a part of an elite team at General Health, Inc. (later acquired by Johnson & Johnson), which pioneered the development of computerized health risk profiles for the workplace. She trained IBM nurses nationwide on using the health appraisal system with IBM employees, an effort that was at the forefront of helping to improve the health of employees.

After graduating from Temple University with an executive master's degree in business administration program, Frisby received the highly selective Certified Financial Planner designation in the early 2000s. As a Black woman, this was a rarity as even today, African Americans make up only 1.8 percent of Certified Financial Planners. Since her retirement, she has been involved in efforts to upgrade New Jersey's voting machines, campaigns encouraging consistent voting, encouraging legislators and her local school board to work on assessing and addressing the mental health needs of Black youth.

John Womble was certainly ahead of his time when it came to teaching Samurai training and all that relates to the original core values, to include the importance of meditation. Though he introduced the practice to his students in 1956, it took the US military almost fifty years to catch up to him—as it was 2004 when the military introduced Samurai meditation as a way to enhance their troops' performance.

Many of Womble's students have turned what they learned from their sensei into lessons to better serve their community as elected officials, police officers, congressional staffers, and federal and state employees. Their accomplishments in the last forty years go beyond the boundaries of the community and affect the health and safety of people around the world. Womble encouraged students to go beyond his accomplishments and improve the system—become better; don't just repeat what others have done—be unique and build on what they learned.

Among his many students, Tyrone Aiken, Steve Potts, John DeLoatch Jr., Keith Pardieck, and Deborah Frisby stand out as the pillars of his legacy. It is through these four exceptionally loyal and committed students that John Womble's legacy can keep inspiring younger generations to embrace the real, original values of Samurai training and apply them to the betterment and the advancement of life conditions, quality, and expectations of the nation as a whole.

INTERLUDE

The March on Washington

"What if they spit on us?" a young woman asked John Womble as they walked toward the Lincoln Memorial in Washington DC.

"I am a Samurai," he said, looking at the endless crowd in front of him. "Nobody is going to spit on us."

It was August 28, 1963, and the energy around them was magnetic, reinvigorating, and thrilling, something that Black America—and the entire nation, for that matter—had never experienced before. The day would go down in history as the March on Washington for Jobs and Freedom.

"You're a Samurai?" she asked.

He nodded and proceeded to briefly tell her about his background.

"But what if they attack us?" she asked, slouching as if to protect herself from something that might have been on the verge of happening. "I saw that a few months ago police attacked demonstrators in Birmingham, Alabama. They used dogs and fire hoses to disperse the crowds. Who says they won't do it here, today, to us?"

Womble turned to look at her. He could see fear in her eyes and knew that he needed to tell her something to calm her down before it took over her mind.

"We have come here in peace today. This is a nonviolent movement, and you are safe with me," he said. "Remember, Samurai never take more than one step back in fighting."

"What does that mean?" she asked.

"I won't let anything bad happen to you," he said. "Do you really think that associates of Dr. Martin Luther King Jr. would have asked me to support the rear of the security detail for the speakers if they didn't trust me or my skills?"

"No, sir," she said, straightening her back as his words breathed reassurance in her. "Sorry about that."

"Don't apologize, just trust me." He looked around and said, "Now I want you to forget about fear, apprehension, and anything else that is keeping your heart hostage. Instead, open your eyes and truly look at what's happening around us. This is a historical moment for all of us, do you see that? We are here to tell our nation, and the whole world, that we want the right to apply for whatever job we know we're qualified for; we want to stay at whatever accommodation we can afford, not just the ones the government has designated for us; we want to eat at whatever restaurant we feel like and enter whatever theater we want to if they're playing a movie that we find interesting. We are here to demand equal voting rights, and not just because we've earned it—such as those of us who served in the US military—but because we are citizens of this country and that is our birthright to decide who represents us in the government. We are here to fulfill the promise of the Emancipation Proclamation that President Abraham Lincoln issued on January 1, 1863. It's time." He paused to ensure that his words were being heard. "This is a day that your children and your great-grandchildren will study in history books. And you will be able to tell them, 'I was there.'"

She took a moment to absorb what was going on around her.

Then said, "One hundred years have gone by since the Emancipation Proclamation." She shook her head in disbelief.

"Yes," he said. "And that's why all the civil rights organizations have come together today. You've already spotted A. Philip Randolph"—he nodded toward the civil rights movement activist—"and Bayard Rustin, one of our most gifted strategists and organizers. Oh, fun story about Rustin. I heard that this morning, at dawn basically, when he came to the Washington Mall, a reporter pointed out how empty the area was and asked if everything was OK. You know, Rustin was the one who had rallied the troops, the one who had made phone calls to all of the civil rights organizations across the country, from his humble office in Harlem, New York, and told them to show up here today. So, when the reporter questioned if everything was fine—which, if you can read between the lines, it means the reporter wanted to know if the march was still going to happen given that only few people were present—Rustin took out a piece of paper, read it, and said: 'Oh yeah, everything is going according to schedule.'" Womble laughed.

"I don't get why it's funny," she said, trying to follow the story.

"The piece of paper was blank!" Womble said, still laughing.

"What!" she said, laughing too. "Did the reporter believe him?"

"He sure did! But if you know anything about Rustin, you know that the man is a jokester. I heard from people who know him well that he's already decided what he wants written on his tombstone."

"What's that?" she asked.

"This [N-Word] Had Fun!"[63]

And the two of them laughed again.

---

[63] Levine, Daniel. *Bayard Rustin and the Civil Rights Movement* (Rutgers University Press, 1999): 248.

"So how many people do you think there are here?" she asked, looking around at the sea of people that surrounded them. All of them were clearly from different walks of life, age, religion, and ethnicity.

"Well, Rustin and the other organizers were hoping for one hundred thousand people," Womble said.

"Do you think they were able to get to that number?"

"Not at all," Womble said.

"Really?" she asked, frowning.

"Look around you," he said. "There are at least two hundred thousand people here!"

It was true: over a quarter of a million people from all over the country had come to the US capital on buses and trains to support the cause and make their voices heard. Their voices came together in the incandescent speeches given by the charismatic orators, culminating with the acclaimed "I Have a Dream" speech by Dr. Martin Luther King Jr.

But what the woman couldn't have possibly known, since she had just met Womble, was that aside from experiencing one of the most important moments in history, she had also witnessed a rather rare event. The man known to his many students for his brevity had been so inspired and empowered by living such a historical moment that he broke out of his usual short sentences and monosyllabic answers. While the whole world listened to the "I Have a Dream" speech, Womble tried to absorb each and every word. Like countless other people, he believed that the March on Washington was indeed the turning point in the history of the United States of America.

As years went by, reality proved to him that historic moments don't equate to immediate changes. Still, he tried holding on to the hope he felt that day, standing among the hundreds of thousands of other hopefuls. It was perhaps that hope, combined with his impeccable Samurai training, that gave him the strength to keep advocating for what was right and standing up for what was important. Even in his final years, he never stopped fighting for social justice. And in true Samurai fashion, he never took more than one step back.

EIGHT

"No man [person] is free who is not master of himself [themselves]"—Epictetus[64]

There is no place for ego in traditional martial arts. There is only room for *giri*, a Japanese word made of two kanji: 義理. Giri can be translated as duty or obligation, but it also embodies the value of loyalty to one's sensei. Giri is deeply rooted in Japanese culture and way of life and does not pertain just to martial arts.

Its origin can be traced back to prefeudal age—though the word itself was first used during medieval times—and it had to with the importance of rice:

> The basis of life among the ancient Japanese was the rice crop. Working conditions were not severe but it was not as easy as just seeding and awaiting a rich harvest. Rice growing required intense cooperative work for short periods, such as during planting and

---

[64] "No man is free who is not master of himself. —Epictetus"
— Master Your Code: The Art, Wisdom, and Science of Leading an Extraordinary Life by Darren J. Gold

harvesting. This kind of labor encouraged the formation of hamlets where people had to cooperate with one another. People who received goodwill from others in the rice field in the form of help in transplanting and reaping rice wanted to return that goodwill, and those who provided the assistance must have expected something in return. In addition, people who lived in the same hamlet must have carefully noted whether they actually received something back. This custom of returning something for goodwill is called *giri* today.[65]

During the Samurai era in Japan, giri was called *go-on to hōkō*, which was a rule "between masters and subordinates in which a 'social and psychological obligation [is] taken on with favors received from others. In reality, *go-on* meant that 'lords granted land to followers,' and *hōkō* that 'the subordinates, feeling on toward their superiors, were inclined to pay them respect and render them loyalty.'"[66]

Loyalty in Samurai training and, later, in martial arts training became one of the most fundamental values in Japanese culture:

In Okinawa, the birthplace of Karate-do, the dōjō is usually at the sensei's home, as the island was not rich and training space was limited. So most of the training was done either in the house, or in the yard. Classes were small, and students were hand-picked by the instructor. It was (and still is) every sensei's aim,

---

[65]   Quoted in Roger J. Davies, *The Japanese Mind: Understanding Contemporary Japanese Culture* (Tuttle Publishing: 2002), 96.

[66]   Davies, *The Japanese Mind*, p. 96.

to produce at least one student (more if possible) to study his complete system, master it, and eventually take over the school - and continue his teacher's art. Therefore, the sensei, who had spent his life mastering his art, would choose a student (or students) to inherit his school, train them in all aspects of Karate-do and that student in return would stay with his teacher, giving him his loyalty and respect, by putting something back into the school. It was a two-way relationship, whereby the teacher would show the student everything he knew. In return the student would always acknowledge his sensei as his teacher, and assist him until he was ready to inherit the school. This is the way that Karate-do is meant to be, like a father/son (or daughter) relationship. The sensei is the "father," the student is the "son" or "daughter." The "father" raises the children in Karate-do, and when they grow up, they either stay with the "father" to help him or, even if they go away, they will always acknowledge their father. And return to him whenever they can.[67]

However, many systems are extinct because the old masters refuse to reveal the secrets of the arts of the Samurai to unworthy students. In fact, Dr. Womble himself used to often say that "not everyone is a suitable vessel for the arts of the Samurai."

The concept of giri has translated into modern Japanese culture as the dedication to keeping harmony within one's community, whether in the form of exchanging gifts of equal value, giving chocolate to

---

[67] Paul Starling, "On-Giri; What is it?" https://www.gojukai.com.au/GIRI_BY_PAUL_STARLING.html

colleagues on Valentine's Day, or being loyal to one's workplace to the point that workers won't consume any products made by their competitors. Individuality is therefore sacrificed for the common good and what's in the best interest of the community one belongs to.

This is a concept hard to grasp for many westerners. One only needs to think of the first-person pronoun "I" that is capitalized in the English language, symbolizing the importance placed on the individual, the ego, and one's own interest as opposed to the community's greater good. This is especially evident when it comes to the many differences between how martial arts are practiced in Japan and how they are practiced in the United States of America. In traditional Japanese martial arts, students' loyalty is to their sensei. They follow one sensei and one school for decades. In the United States of America, on the other hand, it is not uncommon for martial artists to often change martial art schools and, therefore, sensei.

The reason can be found in the emphasis placed in the western world on the importance of winning martial arts competitions as opposed to embracing martial arts as a way of life:

> In the West, many people regard Karate like shopping in a supermarket. They choose some brand, go to the check-out counter and pay for it. ["Here's my $5, now give me $5 worth of Karate"] Then, if they don't like it after a short time, they will try another brand next time. These people don't realize that it takes a lifetime to learn any style of Karate-do (Traditional). [. . .] People who have spent their entire Karate lifetime learning and teaching one style of Karate-do. This leads to the conflict between "sport Karate" and the art of "Karate-do". "Sport Karate" encourages people

to be winners, by defeating others in Kumite or Kata. "Karate-do" teaches that your opponent is yourself, and you must always strive to improve yourself, not necessarily at someone else's expense. Therefore, in Sport Karate - if winning is all that counts - you don't need to stay loyal to your instructor. You can shop and change from one style to another. If you're not winning at that moment under Sensei A, then go and train with Sensei B. Maybe he can help you to win.[68]

Dr. John Womble was a firm believer in Samurai training as a way of life, not as a way to win competitions. His most loyal students have therefore dedicated their entire adult lives to building character, which is the key to resilience. That is the reason why they have been successful in thriving despite facing a pandemic, cancer, record-breaking violence in the country, mental illness, and economic challenges. During the toughest of times, they have never complained and rarely lost composure as their focus was on helping others. The hard training and daily practice that Womble's surviving students go through has often been labeled as fanatical, strange, or alien. While tuning out the rumors and daily belligerent narrative about them, Womble's students have become lifeboats for their community by mentally and spiritually preparing for the unthinkable. Womble's students are aware that tragedy can strike at any given moment, and as such, while their training might appear like a personal hobby, they know they are able to help their community in a time of need. The product of their own legacy, academic, and experience, their minds and bodies adapted to years of immersion in solving the most challenging problems. They

---

[68] Starling, "On-Giri," https://www.gojukai.com.au/GIRI_BY_PAUL_STARLING.html

now live according to principles of the Samurai, whose main goal is to perfect one's character and the ability to control one's own thoughts.

The greatest wish of Dr. Womble's students is to encourage readers to learn more about traditional martial arts that derive from Samurai training, as well as Chinese and Korean systems. It's the critical path of the lessons learned that drives the focus on swaying people's mindset away from the toxic and often self-destructive desire for instant gratification. Dr. Womble's primary sensei, encouraged by the ethos of judo, pioneered tournaments in North America as a character-building opportunity because contests provide students opportunities to test their characters. Even today's elite military organizations recognize the importance of developing character as opposed to singularly focusing on physical training.

To welcome the intangible yet ever-present benefits of Dr. Womble's teaching, it is pivotal to apply less focus to winning competitions just for the sake of medals and trophies and more concentration on the lifelong commitment and dedication that martial arts training requires. Use the concepts of martial arts to motivate yourself to make everyday life interesting and to solve problems in your community. Every day, our actions make us part of the solution or part of the problem in our community.

GLOSSARY

Term	Definition
Akazu-no-mon (ah-kuh-zu no mohn)	A gate located on the east side of the Kumamoto castle, its name meaning "unopened."
Budō (boo-dow)	The parent systems of budō or martial sports is called Bujutsu, the older systems of combat that is not legal to practice outside of military and law enforcement in many countries as it used deadly force to maim or kill with dangerous blows, chock holds, and poison darts.
Bugeisha (boo-gay-shuh)	Student of Bujutsu.
Bujutsu (boo-ju-tsu)	See definition of Budō.

Bun Bu Ichi (boon-boo-ee-tchee)	A Samurai principle that means body and mind in accord.
Bushido (boo-she-dow)	A code of honor followed by Samurai.
Chonmage (ch'on-mah-gheh)	Typical Samurai hairstyle: hair back into a tight topknot.
Chosu (ch'o-soo)	A clan that, along with the Satsuma clan, were vehemently anti-Tokugawa, and joined forces under the name of the fourteen-year-old Emperor Meiji to bring down the Tokugawa shogunate.
Daimyō (dime-yow)	A class of lords ruling over a feudal society; *daimyō* means "great names"
Dōjō (dow-jow)	A room in which people practice martial arts.
Edo (eh-dow)	A historical period in Japan that goes from 1603 to 1867.
Fude (phoo-deh)	Brush used in calligraphy.

Genpei War (Gheh-n-peh-ee)	A war started in 1180 between the Taira and Minamoto clans; it lasted five years and ended with the victory of the Minamoto clan.
Go-Shin-Jutsu (Go-shee-n Joo-tsoo)	An eclectic martial art or a composite of Shaolin and Samurai styles pioneered by Chin Gempin (or Genpin).
Gokai Kaidens (Go-kuh-ee Kh-ee-dens)	Upon graduating at the top of his class, Womble received the Gokai and Jukai Kaidens (fifth and tenth grade Sacred Principles) from his teachers because of his outstanding level of development.
Heian (Hai-uhn)	A period in Japanese history that goes from 794 to 1185
Hideyori (Hee-de-yo-ree)	Toyotomi Hideyoshi's only heir.
Judo (Joo-dow)	A martial art meant to teach character; derived from Jujutsu.
Jukai Kaidens (Joo-kuh-ee Kah-ee-dens)	See "Gokai Kaidens" definition.

Kamishimo (Kah-mee-shee-moh)	Worn by Samurai over the kimono, it consisted of sleeveless jacket and trousers.
Katana (kuh-taa-nuh)	A sword.
Kendo (ken-dow)	A traditional activity in Japan that fostered the fighting spirit.
Kenjutsu (ken-joo-tsu)	The art of the sword, something that Samurai were trained in.
Kimono (kee-mow-now)	Traditional long robes of different colors, decorated with flowers, cranes, or other animals. Usually worn by moth men and women.
Kissaki (kee-suh-kee)	Tip of the sword.
Ko-ryu (koh-ree-uh)	Classical traditions of martial arts that use live weapons and strategic attacks meant to maim, incapacitate, or kill.
Meiji (may-jee)	A period in Japanese history that goes from 1868 to 1912; also known as Imperial Restoration

Menkyo (Men-kee-ow)	License given to a martial arts student when he/she achieves a specific level of expertise.
Modus Vivendi (mow-duhs vuh-ven-dee)	A Latin expression meaning "way of life."
Niten Ichi (nee-ten ee-tchee)	The Samurai skill of using two swords at the same time.
Obi (ow-bee)	A belt worn by Samurai to hold the sword.
Oda Nobunaga (ow-duh now-boo-nuh-gah)	A daimyō and Samurai who wanted to unify Japan and took Yasuke under his wing.
Raijin (ray-jin)	The Shinto god of storm, lightning, and thunder, also known as Kaminari, who protected Japan by creating a divine wind.
Rakkasan (ruhk-kuh-suhn)	A Japanese word meaning "parachute men."
Reigi (ray-ji)	Traditional budō etiquette.
Renzai (rehn-zai)	One of two important Zen Buddhism sects in Japan.

Ronin (row-neehn)	A Samurai without a master.
Ryu (yee-oo)	A Japanese word meaning "school."
Saburau (suh-boo-ruh-oo)	A Japanese word that means "to serve" and the root of the word Samurai
Sensei (sen-say)	Japanese word that refers to a martial arts teacher.
Seppuku (suh-poo-koo)	A ritual suicide that the Samurai performed (also known as Hara-Kiri)
Shaolin (shau-lin)	One of the oldest and most famous styles of Kung Fu.
Shiatsu (shee-aat-soo)	A Japanese form of therapy that involves applying pressure in specific spots on the body.
Shodo (show-dow)	Japanese word that means "the way of writing." Calligraphy was often an indicator of one's social status because, the higher one's class, the more education one pursued.

Shogun (show-guhn)	An all-powerful military commander chosen by the emperor.
Taira (tuhy-ruh)	The Taira clan fought against the Minamoto clan for influence over Japan during the twelfth century.
Tokugawa Ieyasu (tow-koo-gaa-wuh Yay-uh-soo)	Founder of the Tokugawa shogunate, which began in 1603 until 1868.
Toyotomi Hideyoshi (Taa-yuh-tow-mee Hee-duh-yow-shee)	A Samurai who ascended to power in the sixteenth century and exerted tremendous control over the nation by virtue of clever political and military maneuvering.
Yasuke (Yuh-soo-keh)	First Samurai of foreign (non-Japanese) descent.

Professional Karate Association · 9000 Sunset Boulevard · Suite 506 · Los Angeles · California 90069 · (213) 550-8831

September 26, 1977

Dr. Jose Jones
10375 Barcan Circle
Columbia, Md. 21044

Dear Jose:

I just picked up a copy of the most recent issue of Black Belt and
saw John Womble's letter to the editor. Heck, I had no idea he was
a black instructor, Jose, as I couldn't determine that from your
report on the history of D.C. martial arts which you wrote for the
Encyclopedia.

I would really appreciate it if you would extend my sincerest
apologies to Mr. Womble for my error, as it does tend to make him
look bad in front of his students. In fact, if you could forward
this letter to him, he may be able to post it for all his students
to see.

From all the information and data I've been able to gather on the
history of American martial arts, and specifically, karate, I can
safely state that Mr. John Womble is the first known black instructor to teach karate in the United States. His having established
public classes in 1956 predates the efforts of other fine black
instructors such as Mr. Ron Duncan of New York City, and Mr. George
Cofield of Brooklyn. The misinformation contained in my recent
Black Belt series, The Untold Story of American Karate's History,
was an unintentional mistake and will be rectified in the book
I am compiling, The Illustrated Encyclopedia of the Martial Arts.

I want to personally thank Mr. Womble for taking the time to point
out my error so that we can set the record straight once and for
all.

Respectfully,

John Corcoran

John Corcoran

Clarification of who was the first African
American Martial Arts Instructor

3rd Degree Black Belt certification from Master Ki Whang Kim

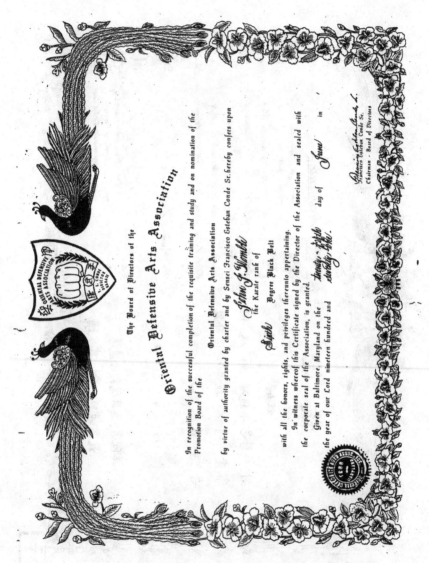

The Board of Directors of the

Oriental Defensive Arts Association

In recognition of the successful completion of the requisite training and study and on nomination of the Promotion Board of the

Oriental Defensive Arts Association

by virtue of authority granted by charter and by Sensei Francisco Esteban Conde Sr. hereby confers upon

John F. Womble

the Karate rank of

Sixth Degree Black Belt

with all the honors, rights, and privileges thereunto appertaining.

In witness whereof this Certificate signed by the Director of the Association and sealed with the corporate seal of the Association, is granted.

Given at Baltimore, Maryland on the twenty-fifth day of June in the year of our Lord nineteen hundred and seventy-five.

Francisco Esteban Conde S.
Chairman - Board of Directors

Sixth Degree Black Belt license granted
from Master Francisco Conde, Sr.

Instructor license from primary Sensei Dr. Chitose with honors.

Defense against dual attack.

Demonstrated by John H DeLaotch, Jr. (L),
Keith Pardieck (C), and Steve Potts (R)

An iconic example of Bun Bu Ichi or Pen and
Sword or Mind and Body in accord.

Maryland Department of Veterans Affairs

Office of the Secretary

ROBERT L. EHRLICH, JR
GOVERNOR

MICHAEL S. STEELE
LT. GOVERNOR

GEORGE W. OWINGS III
SECRETARY

July 22, 2004

Mr. Tyrone Aiken
7822 C Street
Chesapeake Beach, Maryland 20732

Dear Mr. Aiken:

Thank you for your call of June 21 regarding past legislation. I do recall the bill(s), first introduced in 1999, and later when it passed with different sponsors in 2001. I am terribly sorry the FTC did not research the matter to its humble beginnings in our area of the State, but I was not even aware they were creating this award. Frankly, your call was the first I had heard of it. I know you must feel very proud that your idea has helped millions of Americans, even though you did not receive the recognition you deserved.

As you can undoubtedly tell by the new letterhead, I have changed positions and am no longer in the business of preparing legislation as a Delegate. As a point of reference, my replacement is Sue Kullen who will assume her new duties on August 4th. I do not have an address or a number, but know it will be available very shortly. I do wish you the best of luck in all your future endeavors and appreciate having had the opportunity to work with you in the past.

Sincerely,

George W. Owings III
Secretary

THE JEFFREY BUILDING, FOURTH FLOOR
16 FRANCIS STREET, ANNAPOLIS, MARYLAND 21401
TOLL FREE: 866-793-1577 • ANNAPOLIS: 410-260-3838 • FAX: 410-216-7928
www.mdva.state.md.us
TTY USERS CALL VIA MD RELAY

Acknowledging exceptional public service for No Call List.

Council of District of Columbia Resolution

Commendation for Highest Ranking Black Samurai.

Application of Auxiliary Weapon targeting pressure point.

Auxiliary weapon defense against knife attack

Measuring distance from targeted attack to vital target.

Frontal attack and defense

Application of dual auxiliary weapon.

Simultaneously applied defense and offense.

Crucial strike to vital area triggering instant reaction.

Mirroring footwork.

Auxiliary weapons can be used to deflect
and defend simultaneously.

Kata execution with precision.

Forcefully defending against momentous attack.

Anticipation of attack from rear.

Redirecting force of attack.

Equal application of force to model realistic attack.

Blending while delivering final strike.

Triangulation applied to deliver sufficient
force to neutralize attacker.

GERRY SIKORSKI, MINNESOTA, CHAIRMAN

JAMES P. MORAN, JR., VIRGINIA,   CONSTANCE A. MORELLA, MARYLAND
VICE CHAIRMAN   THOMAS J. RIDGE, PENNSYLVANIA
ELEANOR HOLMES NORTON,
DISTRICT OF COLUMBIA

U.S. House of Representatives

COMMITTEE ON POST OFFICE AND CIVIL SERVICE

SUBCOMMITTEE ON THE CIVIL SERVICE

122 CANNON HOUSE OFFICE BUILDING

Washington, DC 20515-6244

TELEPHONE (202) 225-4025

November 14, 1991

The Honorable William Reilly
Administrator
Environmental Protection Agency
401 M Street S.W.
Washington, DC 20460

Dear Administrator Reilly:

Pursuant to Rule X and XI of the House of Representatives and Rule 22(4) and 24 of the House Committee on Post Office and Civil Service, the Subcommittee on the Civil Service, House Committee on Post Office and Civil Service, has the responsibility for conducting oversight activities into matters affecting civil servants, the welfare of the civil service system, and the implementation of equal employment opportunity principles in the Federal government.

The Subcommittee derives its authority to conduct hearings into matters affecting civil servants from Committee Rule 24. It provides for the following: "Each Subcommittee is authorized to meet, hold hearings, conduct investigations, receive evidence, and report to the committee on all matters referred to it..."

Pursuant to this responsibility, the Subcommittee will hold a legislative hearing on HR 3613, the Federal Employee Fairness Act, on Wednesday, November 20, 1991, at 10:00 A.M. in 2175 Rayburn House Office Building. We respectfully request that the Department make Mr. Tyrone Aiken, Chemist in the Office of Pesticide Programs, available to testify before the Subcommittee in Washington D.C. at that time.

Mr. Aiken is being invited to testify pursuant to the Committee's legislative jurisdiction. Past Subcommittee experience indicates that when civil servants testify before Congress in their individual capacity, retaliation may occur. Under the Lloyd LaFollette Act, codified at 5 U.S.C. 7211,

The right of employees... to furnish information to either House of Congress, or to a committee or Member thereof, may not be interfered with... denied.

Moreover, the obstruction of Congress statute, 18 U.S.C. sec. 1505, provides that "Whoever... corruptly . . . endeavors to

influence, obstruct or impede . . . the due and proper exercise of
the power of inquiry . . . [of] any committee of either
House . . . .Shall be fined not more than $5,000 or imprisoned not
more than five years, or both." The legislative history of this
statute and the obstruction of justice statute make it clear that
forcing employees out of a job, or otherwise damaging them in their
employment, to influence testimony or as retaliation for testimony
afterwards, can be a violation of this criminal statute.

We know you and your senior officials would not even consider
violating these statutes. However, as the Subcommittee which
oversees the civil service statutes, we are unfortunately aware
that in the course of these investigations, subordinate officials
in agencies in which our witnesses work, who may have strong
feelings about our investigations, do not always take every step
to avoid the appearance of activity in violation of these statutes.
In particular, the appearance of activity in violation of these
statutes can occur when a witness who has been requested to testify
before Congress is questioned by his or her superiors or by other
agency personnel about that testimony, either before or after the
appearance. Additionally, personnel actions adverse to the witness
before or after testimony may be suspect as retaliatory in nature.

The Subcommittee has a strong legislative interest in
potentially retaliatory acts. Accordingly, I would ask that if any
consideration is given by agency personnel to talking to our
witnesses regarding their testimony or regarding our investigation,
that we receive advance notice of who is considering this, and what
they are considering. We would most certainly want to know if any
plans to talk to our witnesses were consummated. Please take the
necessary steps to see that subordinate officials are made aware
of these concerns and that the Subcommittee receives full advance
notice, and complete information, if any agency personnel consider
any steps of such a nature.

Your cooperation in this matter is greatly appreciated.

Sincerely,

CONSTANCE MORELLA
Ranking Member

GERRY SIKORSKI
Chairman

cc: Mr. Aiken

Congressional warning to US EPA about retaliation against
Tyrone Aiken (employee) for testifying before Congress.

Defense against Knife attack.

Using auxiliary weapon to launch surprise attack.

The Tang of 400-year-old Golden Sword.

Demonstrated by Tyrone R. Aiken

Justice

Demonstrated by Tyrone R. Aiken

Compassion

Demonstrated by Tyrone R. Aiken

Self-Control

Demonstrated by Tyrone R. Aiken

Honor

Demonstrated by Tyrone R. Aiken

Courage

Demonstrated by Tyrone R. Aiken

Honesty

Demonstrated by Tyrone R. Aiken

Loyalty

Demonstrated by Tyrone R. Aiken

Respect

Printed in the United States
by Baker & Taylor Publisher Services